Excel®

PORTABLE GENIUS

by Lisa A. Bucki

WILEY

SKY10022068_110220

Excel®

PORTABLE GENIUS

About the Author

An author, trainer, and content expert, **Lisa A. Bucki** has been educating others about computers, software, business, and personal growth topics since 1990. She has written and contributed to dozens of books and multimedia works, in addition to providing marketing and training services to her clients and writing online tutorials. Bucki is co-founder of 1x1 Media, LLC (www.1x1media.com), an independent publisher of books and courses focused on how-to topics for entrepreneurs, startup founders, makers, and other business professionals.

Acknowledgments

When Associate Publisher Jim Minatel reached out to me to ask if I was still writing, I was thrilled. I had been off in the wilderness working on other types of projects, so signing on with Wiley felt like a return to my publishing roots. It even got better from there. When he and Senior Managing Editor Pete Gaughan brought Project Manager Kezia Endsley and Technical Editor Joyce Nielsen on board, it was (as Jim put it) "fun getting the band back together." All of us have worked together in various capacities and projects going back decades. And all of my colleagues on this project are still at the top of their game.

I thank all of them for their excellent work on this project, as well as Copy Editor Kim Wimpsett, Content Refinement Specialist Saravanan Dakshinamurthy, Proofreader Nancy Carrasco, and all the other Wiley employees or partners who had a direct or indirect role in this undertaking.

My gratitude also eternally flows to my excellent and patient husband, Steve Poland, and all of our beloved furry dog children.

Contents

chapter 1

How Do I Start Using Excel?   2

chapter 2

How Do I Make Changes to My Sheet? 30

chapter 3

How Do I Add Up the Numbers with Formulas? 54

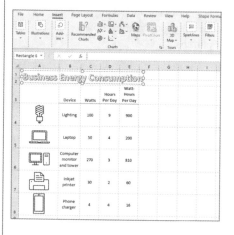

chapter 7

How Do I Manage Lists of Information?

chapter 8

How Do I Present My Data in Charts?

chapter 9

How Do I Print and
Share My Content? 194

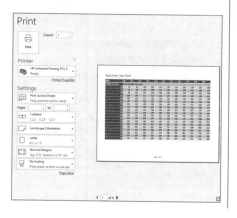

Index 212

Introduction

If having hundreds of millions of users or more constitutes success, then Excel meets that test. In my decades as a tech writer and editor, Excel has led the competition in providing powerful yet accessible computational and data capabilities. "Accessible" can be a relative term, however. For some people, the hundreds of features in Excel can be intimidating. Others may wrestle with the best ways to create formulas or manage lists of data.

Excel Portable Genius aims to help you answer nine key questions you may come up against when using Excel. The book covers the Excel features that you *need* to know, along with some others that you should *want* to know. I try to get right to the point in describing features and steps, so you can power through, problem-solve on your own, and free up time for other activities.

A few special elements provide guardrails and inspiration. Notes help you delve a bit deeper into some topics, Cautions give advice and help you steer clear of problems, and Genius icons convey the pro tips that will make you more efficient, more productive, and (I daresay) more impressive in the results that you crank out from Excel.

I need to mention one last item from the "need to know" category before you dive in to Chapter 1. The screenshots for the figures in this book were shot at a low 1024 x 768 resolution to enhance their final appearance within the book's format. Most users now have their screens set to a much higher resolution, so you may see differences in your screen versus the figures, particularly with regard to the appearance of the ribbon. Also, users with touch screen systems may see additional screen options and features not shown in the figures.

Thank you, reader, for adding *Excel Portable Genius* to your library.

How Do I Start Using Excel?

AutoSave ● Off | Order Summary.xlsx - Saved ▾ | Lisa Bucki

File | Home | Insert | Page Layout | Formulas | Data | Review | View | Help

Calibri | 11 | General | Conditional Formatting ˅ | Insert ˅
B I U ˅ A^ A˅ | $ ˅ % , | Format as Table ˅ | Delete ˅
Paste | .00 .0 | Cell Styles ˅ | Format ˅

Clipboard | Font | Alignment | Number | Styles | Cells | Editin

E15

	A	B	C	D	E	F
1	Order Summary					
2	Operator:	name@example.com				
3						
4	Order #	Date	Customer	Total	Disc. %	
5	1	6/20/2023	Ryan	99.99	15%	
6	2	6/20/2023	Miller	129.99	10%	
7	3	6/24/2023	Smith	80.95	10%	
8	4	6/28/2023	Acton	65.25	5%	
9	5	6/29/2023	Ryan	349.58	15%	
10	6	6/29/2023	Casper	79.99	5%	
11	7	6/30/2023	Smith	58.75	10%	
12	8	6/30/2023	Phillips	275.89	5%	
13	9	6/30/2023	Yelton	105.75	5%	
14	10	7/1/2023	Miller	79.99	10%	
15						

Order Summary | Sheet2 | Sheet3 | +

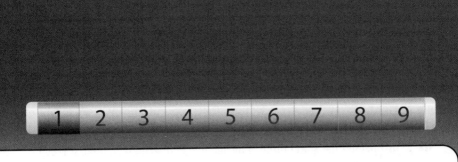

Excel has a lot in common with other programs you may have used, including the other Microsoft 365 applications. Its interface is easy to navigate yet loaded with powerful features designed to save you time and work. Getting dialed in on all the basics will enable you to spend more of your time analyzing the meaning of your data, which is the important thing, right? This chapter introduces you to the "must know" skills for kicking off your work in Excel. It covers essential command and navigation features of the user interface, reviews key techniques for creating and working with files, and guides you through getting data into sheet cells and making selections.

Starting and Exiting Excel

Windows 10 gives you a few options for starting a program so that you can get to work. You may already have your preference for how to start up, but if not, you can try one of these methods:

- **Start button.** Click the Start button at the left end of the Windows taskbar. Move the mouse pointer over the right edge of the list of programs in the Start menu so that a scroll bar expands, and then use the scroll bar or the scroll wheel on your mouse to scroll down until you see Excel in the list. Then choose Excel. You also can pin a larger tile for starting Excel to the right side of the Start menu. Right-click Excel in the list of Start menu programs, and choose Pin to Start. Then you can open the Start menu and click the large tile. If you need to remove the tile later, right-click it and and choose Unpin from Start.

- **Windows logo key.** Press the Windows logo key on your keyboard. Press the down arrow on your keyboard as needed until Excel is selected, and then press Enter.

- **Search box.** Click in the Search box to the right of the Start button on the taskbar. If a tile for Excel appears in the Top Apps section, click it. If not, start typing **Excel**, and then choose Excel App when it appears under Best Match, as shown in Figure 1.1.

All	Apps	Documents	Web	More ▼		2835

Best match

X **Excel**
   App

Apps

○ Internet Explorer >

File Explorer >

Search the web

🔍 Ex - See web results >

X

Excel
App

☐ Open

1.1 Select Excel App when using Windows Search to start Excel.

Genius

If using the Start menu to launch Excel isn't for you, then you can pin an Excel button to the taskbar. With Excel open, right-click its button on the taskbar, and then choose Pin to Taskbar. Click the pinned Excel button on the taskbar to start the program. If you decide you want to unpin the button, right-click it on the taskbar and choose Unpin from Taskbar.

When Excel opens, it prompts you to create a new document or open an existing one. The later section called "Working with Files" provides more details about those choices. For now, you could just click the Blank Workbook thumbnail to create a new file.

When you've finished all your work in Excel for the day, you should close or exit the program. You could shut down Windows without closing Excel, but it's a better practice to close Excel first to ensure you've saved all your work. As when starting Excel, you have these options for closing or exiting the program:

- Click the Close (X) button at the upper-right corner of the screen.
- Press Alt+F4.

To close the current file without exiting Excel, click the File tab near the upper-left corner of the Excel window, and then choose Close. If you have a file with unsaved work open and exit Excel or close the file, a message box asks whether you want to save changes to the file. You can click the Save or Don't Save button as needed.

> **!** **Caution** If you have multiple Excel files open, closing one of them doesn't close down Excel overall. You have to close every open Excel file to make sure you've completely exited the program.

Taking a Look Around

When you're writing a document in a word processor, you can get away with just typing a lot and not knowing the nuances of how to get around. Excel is trickier than that. Some of the features of its interface are important to being able to work accurately in the program, especially when it comes to creating formulas that calculate or organizing data effectively. While some of what this section covers may seem familiar based on your work with other programs, especially other Microsoft 365 programs, you might learn about a few unique Excel interface features that offer powerful shortcuts.

Reviewing key screen features

At first glance, the Excel screen can look a bit busy with an extreme number of buttons and letters and numbers and boxes. Each sheet in an Excel file has more than 16,000 columns and 1,000,000 rows, for a total of more than 17 billion cells! That sounds overwhelming, so I'm going to zero in on the key screen features you need to know to work in Excel, which are shown in Figure 1.2. Later parts of the book will cover other features of the Excel interface in discussions about particular tasks and actions.

Labels pointing to the Excel screenshot:
- Quick Access Toolbar (QAT)
- Ribbon tabs
- Title bar
- Dialog box launcher
- Formula bar
- Column letters
- Ribbon group
- Active cell
- Row numbers
- Mouse pointer
- Sheet tab
- Status bar

1.2 You will work with these tools in Excel.

Here's what you need to know about the screen features shown in Figure 1.2:

- **Title bar.** The title bar identifies the name of the current file and holds other tools at its left and right end.

- **Quick Access Toolbar.** Found at the left end of the title bar, the Quick Access Toolbar (QAT) offers Save, Undo, and Redo buttons by default. The Undo and Redo buttons become active after you start performing actions in cells. Clicking the down arrow at the right end of the QAT opens the Customize Quick Access Toolbar menu, where you can choose the name of another button that you want to add to the QAT.

● **Ribbon.** The ribbon below the title bar uses tabs to organize the majority of the commands that you'll use in Excel. Click a ribbon tab to see its commands. The names along the bottom of the ribbon identify commands that are grouped together because they have related or similar functions. In most cases, you click a button on the ribbon to choose a command, though clicking a button with a drop-down list arrow on it opens a list of additional choices. Still other ribbon buttons are split, with both a regular button on the top and a down arrow on the bottom part of the button. Clicking the top half of a split button executes the command immediately, while clicking the bottom part with the arrow opens a list of choices. Other buttons are split the other way, with the main button on the left and a drop-down list arrow on the right. Pressing the Alt key displays letters and numbers, sometimes called *keytips*, that you can press to choose a ribbon tab and then a command.

Note

I'll use a type of shorthand throughout the book to tell you which ribbon command to choose, giving the tab, group, and specific button. For example, if I say "Choose Data ➔ Sort & Filter ➔ Filter," it means to click the Data tab on the ribbon, look for the Sort & Filter group of commands, and in that group, click Filter. Command sequences can be longer if a list or menu appears.

● **Dialog box launcher.** Some groups on the ribbon include a small button called a *dialog box launcher* in the lower-right corner. Clicking one of these buttons opens a dialog box with more detailed choices, such as the Format Cells dialog box.

● **Formula bar.** You will use this area to enter and edit cell contents. The Formula bar also displays the contents of the active cell. Or, if the active cell contains a formula, the formula appears in the Formula bar, while the formula results appear in the cell itself.

● **Row numbers and column letters.** The working area in Excel is organized into rows and columns of cells. The column letters across the top of the grid and the row numbers down the left side identify the address or location of a cell or range. The bands with the letters and numbers are also called *row and column headers*.

● **Active cell.** A bold outline, sometimes called the *cell selector*, identifies the active or currently selected cell. When more than one cell is selected, the bold box surrounds the entire selection.

● **Mouse pointer.** When you're using the mouse in Excel, the mouse pointer changes shape often to cue you when it's in the correct position to perform a particular action. By default, the pointer shape is a bold white plus, as shown in Figure 1.2, but at times it may change to a black plus, a two-headed arrow, and other shapes.

- **Sheet tab.** A tab appears for each worksheet in the file. The later section "Working with Sheets" explains how to add and work with sheets.

- **Status bar.** This area below the worksheet displays status information and has tools for changing the zoom that I'll cover shortly.

Note

The more recent subscription versions of Excel have made it easier to get help when you're stuck with a feature or task. Make sure your computer is connected to the Internet to receive the best possible results, and then press F1 or choose Help → Help → Help to open a Help pane at the right side of Excel. Enter a command name, task, or other search keywords, and then press Enter to see matching results.

Workbooks versus worksheets

Excel files are called workbook files, though you may see them called *documents* like the files created using other Microsoft 365 applications. The more specific name, *workbook*, stems from how Excel enables you to organize your data in an orderly fashion on separate worksheets or sheets, each of which is represented by a sheet tab at the bottom-left corner of Excel. Just as it's easier to organize and find information in a booklet with pages rather than a long, continuous scroll, placing sets of data on separate worksheets gives you faster access to your data.

Before you make your first entries in a new workbook file, take a few extra minutes to plan in your mind how you'd like to organize the data in the file. For example, you typically wouldn't want to combine both sales and inventory data on a single sheet. More typically, you would place the sales data on one worksheet, and the inventory data on another. For large datasets, sales and inventory might even be tracked in separate workbook files. Let the type of data dictate how you organize it. In a workbook file tracking weather data, each month's data could be placed on a separate sheet. A workbook file with real estate listings might have the listings for each ZIP code on a separate tab. A construction business might place each project estimate for a client on a separate sheet.

Changing views

The View tab on the ribbon (Figure 1.3) enables you to change the view in Excel and turn some view features on and off. The default view, Normal, was shown in Figure 1.2. If you have a sheet that you want to print and think you might need to adjust how it breaks between separate pages, change to the Page Break Preview view. The Page Layout view not only shows page breaks, but it also shows how headers and footers will appear when printed. The Workbook Views group of the View tab holds the buttons for changing to one of these views. Three buttons near the right end of the status bar also enable you to change between the views.

1.3 Use the View tab choices to adjust screen appearance.

The Show group of the View tab has Formula Bar, Gridlines, and Headings check boxes that you can use to toggle those screen features on and off. (*Headings* is another name for row and column headers.) When you want to finalize a workbook file and discourage other people from making edits, you might click the Formula Bar check box to uncheck it, thus hiding the Formula bar. It's common to turn off the gridlines and headings displays for some types of worksheets, such as an executive dashboard that shows summary information and a few charts. In particular, hiding the gridlines makes some sheets more readable and attractive. Keep in mind that these settings in the Show group of the View tab control only on-screen display of gridlines and headers. If you want to control whether gridlines and headers print, you'll have to adjust the page setup, which is covered in Chapter 9.

> **Note** The tools in the Sheet View group of the View tab only become active when you're working on a workbook file stored in a OneDrive, OneDrive for Business, and SharePoint location. You can use the New Sheet View button to create a custom view of a shared workbook file. The custom view enables you to work without disruption, no matter what someone else working on the shared file does.

Another aspect of Excel's on-screen appearance that you might want to tinker with is whether the ribbon is fully visible. The small up arrow button in the lower-right corner of the ribbon is called the Collapse the Ribbon button. You can click it or press Ctrl+F1 to hide everything but the ribbon tabs, allowing more sheet rows to appear on-screen. When you need to choose a command, just click a tab to expand the ribbon temporarily, choose the desired button or item, and then continue working. The ribbon will collapse again on its own. To return the ribbon to its normal appearance and function, click a ribbon tab, and then click the Pin the Ribbon button—it has a pushpin on it—in the lower-right corner of the ribbon or press Ctrl+F1 again. You also can double-click a ribbon tab to collapse the ribbon or pin it back open.

Zooming

Today's trend of computers offering ever-higher screen resolutions has its pros and cons. While graphics and video look gorgeous in hi-res, screen features and content in business-oriented programs can look small and difficult to read. Whether you've forgotten your glasses or just have eyestrain from a full day of screen time, increasing the zoom or zooming in can make sheet data easier to read. On the other hand, decreasing the zoom or zooming out allows more rows and columns to appear on-screen at once, which can be handy in some situations, such as when you need to select a large set of data for a chart.

The Zoom group of the View tab holds choices for changing the zoom. You can select an area on the worksheet, and then click the Zoom to Selection button in that group so the selection will fill the screen, usually by zooming in. To return to the normal zoom, click the 100% button in the group. Clicking the Zoom button opens the Zoom dialog box, which enables you to choose a preset zoom percentage or enter your own setting in the Custom text box; click OK to apply your choice and close the dialog box.

You also can use the Zoom slider shown in Figure 1.4 to change the zoom on the fly. You can drag the slider "thumb" to the left to zoom out or to the right to zoom in. Or, you can click the Zoom Out (-) or Zoom In (+) buttons at either end of the slider to zoom out or in at preset 10% increments. When you change the zoom using any method, the change normally applies to the current sheet only. Note that Figure 1.4 also shows the status bar buttons for changing the view.

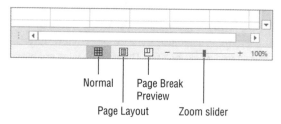

Normal | Page Break Preview

Page Layout | Zoom slider

1.4 These controls at the right end of the status bar enable you to change the view and zoom.

Genius

A zoom setting of 120–125% strikes a good compromise between increasing the zoom enough to reduce eyestrain while still allowing plenty of rows and columns to appear on-screen at once.

Working with Files

Now that you've had an overview of how Excel ticks, it's time to turn to the practical business of starting to work with files. When you click the File tab on the ribbon, a screen loaded primarily with choices for working with files appears. This screen is sometimes called Backstage or Backstage view. You can use the choices on the File tab to create, save, export, and print files, among other actions.

Creating a blank file

You learned at the start of the chapter that when you start Excel, it prompts you to open or create a file. You can click the Blank Workbook thumbnail to create a new, blank file at that point. If you've already started Excel and opened a file (blank or otherwise), you can choose File → Blank Workbook (Figure 1.5) to create another blank file. But for my money, it's fastest to press Ctrl+N to create a new file. No matter the method, Excel assigns a placeholder name (Book1, Book2, and so on) to each blank file you create until you save it under a new name.

⊖	**Good afternoon**
⌂ Home	∨ New
🗋 New	
🗁 Open	Blank workbook · Take a tour (Welcome to Excel) · Drop-down tutorial (Create a Drop-down list)
Info	
Save	
Save As	
Print	🔍 Search

1.5 Choose File → Blank Workbook to create a new, blank workbook file.

Caution If you work in Excel for the web, the cloud-based version of Excel, you might have gotten very comfortable with how it automatically saves the file for you as you work. Unfortunately, the desktop version of Excel isn't as helpful, so you should make sure you save your work frequently. See the later section called "Saving and Closing a File" to learn how to save.

Exploring templates

If starting from a blank slate sounds like too much work, if you're looking for worksheet design ideas, or if you're fairly certain someone else has already created just the type of file you're looking for, then you might just find what you need in the huge selection of templates offered through Excel. A template is simply a pre-made file that typically includes labels, placeholder content or prompts, formulas, and formatting. When you use a template file, which has a slightly different file format than a regular workbook file, it creates a new workbook file with the same contents as the template for you. You fill it out with your own content from there and save the copied file. Thousands of business and personal templates are available for download, including planners, calendars, budgets, invoices, and inventory lists.

To find and download a template, follow these steps:

1. **Choose File → New.** The options for creating a new file appear.

2. **Scroll down to see thumbnails for suggested templates.**

3. **Click a template thumbnail to select it.** As shown in Figure 1.6, a larger preview of the template appears, along with a description and the download size information.

1.6 You get to preview a template before downloading it.

4. **If the template looks like what you want, click the Create button.** The template downloads to your computer, and a new file based on the template opens in Excel. You can then add your own content and save the copy of the template file.

If you didn't see a template that looked promising in Step 2, you can scroll back up and click one of the Suggested Searches choices under the Search for Online Templates text box. Or, you could click in that text box, type a search term or brief description, and press Enter. Excel displays thumbnails for matching templates in its search results. At that point, you could continue with Step 3 to select and download a template.

Caution

The templates you download through Excel are from a trusted source, so they should be free from viruses. If you obtain a template from another source, make sure to check it for viruses and other malware.

Excel automatically stores each template you download into a subfolder of your Windows 10 user folder so that you can reuse it. The next time you choose File → New, downloaded templates will appear at the top of the screen to the right of the Blank Workbook thumbnail. If you've downloaded numerous templates, you may have to click an arrow button to scroll right to find the one that you'd like to reuse. To remove a template from the choices at the top of the screen, right-click it and choose Remove from List.

Opening an existing file

When you start Excel or click the File tab, the initial screen that appears includes a Recent list, which includes previously saved files you've worked in during the not-too-distant past. Click a file in that list to open it immediately.

If the file to open is not on the Recent list, click the Open choice at the left (below New). Toward the middle of the screen, a list of locations appears. Depending on the type of Microsoft 365 subscription you have, there might be OneDrive and Sites locations for cloud-based storage. You can choose a location like that to look for files.

Lower, under Other Locations, the This PC and Browse choices appear. If you click This PC, the list at the right changes to show the files in the same folder as the currently opened file (if any). You can use the up arrow button to the left of the folder breadcrumb trail at the top to navigate a bit and display different files.

I prefer to click Browse and use the good old Open dialog box (Figure 1.7) to navigate to the location holding a file and open it. As shown in Figure 1.7, when you move the mouse pointer over the Navigation pane at the left, arrows appear to the left of the listed locations so that you can expand and collapse the listing. Clicking the right arrow beside This PC would show all the storage locations under This PC, including available disk drives on your computer. Double-click an item in the Navigation pane to show its contents in the file list at the middle of the dialog box. If you need to open a folder from the file list, double-click it. The Address box at the top of the dialog box shows the path to the current folder. When the file you want to open appears in the file list, either double-click it or click it and click the Open button.

Navigation pane   Folder path

Open							×
← → ∨ ↑	« Documents › Work › Wiley			∨ Ö	🔎 Search Wiley		
Organize ▾ New folder						▤ ▾ ▯	❓
	Name ˄		Date modified		Type		
∨ ⭐ Quick access	🔲 Sales by Location.xlsx		6/28/2020 3:09 PM		Microsoft Excel W...		
🖥 Desktop 📌							
⬇ Downloads 📌							
📄 Documents 📌							
🖼 Pictures 📌							
› 🟢 Microsoft Excel							
› ☁ OneDrive							
› 🖥 This PC							
∨ 🖧 Network							
› 🖥 DESKTOP-NVI0H	‹					›	

File name: [   ] ∨   All Excel Files (*.xl*;*.xlsx;*.xlsm ∨)

Tools ▾   Open ▾   Cancel

1.7 Use the Open dialog box to locate and open an existing file.

Genius

Glitches happen. Your laptop might lose power and shut down before you saved your file, or the system might restart on you after a Windows update installed in the background. To try to recover an unsaved file in Excel, choose File → Open. Below the list of files at the right, click the Recover Unsaved Workbooks button. The Open dialog box that appears lists any unsaved files. Click the file to reopen, and then click the Open button.

Switching to another file

While it's possible for a huge amount of data to "live" in a single Excel workbook file, in practice you'd make life a bit rough on yourself to jam a file so full of sheets and cell entries that you can't find what you need when you need it. That said, even when you follow best practices and maintain a focused scope for the content in each of your workbook files, you may encounter situations where you need to be working with two or more files at once. You might need to copy some information from one workbook to another, or you might want to view a formula you created in one file to refresh your memory while creating a similar formula in another file, among other reasons.

With the needed files open, you can use the View tab shown in Figure 1.3 to switch to another file when needed. On the View tab, click the Switch Windows button in the Window group, and then click the name of the file. If you like using the taskbar, you can move the mouse pointer over the Excel button. When a thumbnail for each open file appears, click the desired thumbnail. To use the keyboard to display another file, press and hold the Alt key, briefly press the Tab key while still holding Alt, use the arrow keys to select the thumbnail for the file to display, and then release the Alt key.

Another method is not really "switching" files exactly. You can change the size and position of Excel windows on-screen, such as when you might want to be able to see data from two files at the same time. The Minimize and Restore Down/Maximize buttons sit to the left of the Close (X) button in the upper-right corner of each Excel window, as shown in Figure 1.8.

Here's how those buttons work and come into play when working with multiple files:

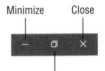

Minimize   Close

Restore Down/Maximize

1.8 You can also work with a window's size and position to facilitate working with multiple files.

- ⊙ **Minimize.** Clicking this button collapses the file down to the Excel taskbar button, effectively switching you to the next open Excel file.

- ⊙ **Restore Down/Maximize.** A window is maximized when it fills the computer screen, and clicking this button on a maximized window reduces the window to a smaller (but still visible) size. The button changes from Restore Down to Maximize when the window is not maximized. In a situation where you need to see information in two separate files at the same time, click the Restore Down button for each window. To resize each window, move the mouse pointer over the window border so that it changes to a white double-headed arrow, and then drag until the window reaches the dimensions you want. Then drag each window by its title bar to position it on-screen as desired. Click the Maximize button to return a window to full screen size.

Note

The Window group of the View tab offers additional choices for viewing and sizing workbook windows, such as Arrange All, which opens a dialog box with choices for arranging the open windows. You also can right-click the Windows taskbar and use some of its choices, such as Show Windows Side by Side, to arrange the open windows. Keep in mind, though, that the taskbar shortcut menu choices apply to open windows from all programs.

Making Your First Cell Entries

The intersection of a row and column in Excel forms a cell that can hold an entry. The column letter and row number combined identify the *cell address*, also called the *cell reference*. For example, the address for the cell in column C of row 9 is C9. Knowing the cell address comes in handy when you need to jump to a particular piece of information in a worksheet, as well as when you are building formulas.

Excel holds a few surprises for you when you're moving around and making different types of cell entries. I'll highlight the shortcuts and the pitfalls for you.

Moving around the sheet

When you move around the worksheet, you change the cell that's the active cell. Any entry that you make will then appear in the active cell, which is why I'm covering moving around as a prelude to making cell entries. The most obvious way to move around a worksheet is to press the down, up, left, and right arrow keys, moving the cell selector one cell in the arrow direction. Or, you can click a cell that appears on-screen to make it active immediately.

Genius

If you know the address for a cell that doesn't currently appear on-screen that you want to select, press Ctrl+G or choose Home → Editing → Find & Select → Go To. In the Reference text box of the Go To dialog box, type the cell address, and then click OK. Boom, cell selected!

You also can use the scroll bars to change the area of the worksheet currently displayed on-screen. The vertical scroll bar at the right controls up and down movement, and the horizontal scroll bar at the bottom controls left and right movement. Figure 1.9 shows these scroll bars. Drag the scroll box in the scroll bar to move more quickly, or click an arrow at either end of the bar to move in smaller increments. And—this is important— moving with the scroll bars does not change the active cell. So after you use a scroll bar, be sure to click the cell you need to select.

Vertical scroll bar —————

Horizontal scroll bar

1.9 Use the scroll bars to display another section of the worksheet.

My other favorite keyboard shortcuts for moving around in Excel include the PgUp and PgDn keys, which move the active cell up or down by one screenful of rows. (Keep in mind that the number of rows may vary depending on your zoom setting and row heights in the sheet.) I also like Ctrl+End, which selects the cell at the bottom-right corner of the range that holds data on the sheet, and Ctrl+Home, which jumps back to cell A1.

Caution If the PgUp and PgDn keys on your keyboard are integrated with a 10-key keypad, you must press the Num Lk (Number Lock) button to turn off having the keys enter numbers and activate the alternate functions of the keys. Press Num Lk again to return to number entry.

Text and values

Once you've selected a cell, you can type in various types of information. This section covers the most basic types of entries, while Chapters 3 and 4 will cover how to enter and create formulas—a topic whose scope requires two chapters. After you type an entry in a cell, to finish the entry and select the next cell, press Enter if you want to move down the column or press Tab if you want to move across the row. Keep these notes about the different types of entries in mind as you begin to populate a worksheet with data:

- **Text.** Also called labels, text entries can serve as items in a list of data, column or row headings and other types of identifiers, or notes or instructions on the sheet. Excel considers any alphanumeric entry that begins with a letter to be text. Text entries can include entries that begin with a number, such as 10 Handbags or A123. By default, text entries align to the left in the cell.

> **!**
>
> **Caution**
>
> Excel's AutoCorrect feature automatically fixes some text entry typos, as well as some entries that aren't typos. For example, if you enter EHR, the acronym for "electronic health records," AutoCorrect changes it to HER. Similarly, WOH, which might stand for "work on hand," gets changed to WHO. You can edit the entry to fix unwanted corrections. Choose File ➔ Options, click Proofing at the left side of the Excel Options dialog box, and then click AutoCorrect Options to adjust these corrections.

- **Values.** These are the numeric entries you make in a sheet and are typically the values used to perform calculations. By default, value entries align to the right in the cell. If you have an instance where you need for Excel to store a numeric entry as text, type a ' (single quote) at the start of the entry.

- **Hyperlinks.** If you type a website address or email address into a cell, Excel automatically converts it to a hyperlink. You can click the hyperlink in a cell (when you see the hand mouse pointer over the hyperlink) to open the linked web page or create a new email message to a contact. You have to click and hold on the cell to select the cell itself. Note that you also can insert other types of hyperlinks, such as a link to a contract or other relevant resource document, by pressing Ctrl+K or choosing Insert ➔ Links ➔ Link (choose the top part of the Link button) and then using the Insert Hyperlink dialog box to select the file to link.

Figure 1.10 shows examples of text, value, and hyperlink entries in a sheet. Any entry that is too long to fit in its cell automatically spills over into the next cell to the right, like the email address entered in cell B2. Chapter 5 will present a few techniques for addressing how entries fit in cells, such as increasing the column width. Excel also provides shortcuts for entering series of information. See "Using Auto Fill and Filling Series" in Chapter 2 to learn more.

E4	▼	:	✕	✓	*fx*	Disc. %	

◢	A	B	C	D	E	F
1	Order Summary					
2	Operator:	name@example.com				
3						
4	Order #	Date	Customer	Total	Disc. %	
5	1		Ryan			
6	2		Miller			
7	3		Smith			
8	4		Acton			
9	5		Ryan			
10	6		Casper			
11	7		Smith			
12	8		Phillips			
13	9		Yelton			
14	10		Miller			
15						

1.10 You can make basic entries like these in sheet cells.

Genius

Despite that little inconvenience of sometimes having to toggle Num Lk on and off, I love having a 10-key keypad on my laptop or keyboard to speed up numeric data entry in Excel. It's much easier to use the compact keypad layout than to stretch for the number keys near the top of the keyboard, especially if you've had any 10-key typing training. If you're a heavy Excel user looking to up your data entry game, check out some online 10-key tutorials.

Dates and times

Excel treats dates and times differently than other types of entries. It converts each date or time entry into a date serial number behind the scenes, even though the date and time continues to display as usual in the cell. Because it stores dates as serial numbers, you can create formulas to do date-related actions, such as finding out how many days fall between a start date and an end date. As a practical matter, you don't have to worry about the serial number. All you have to do is type the date, time, or a combination of the two in a format that Excel recognizes and then press Enter or Tab. Figure 1.11 shows examples of acceptable date and time entries. Don't forget to include AM or PM when you're typing a time according to the regular 12-hour clock. In some cases, Excel automatically changes the width of the column when you make one or more date entries.

19

B14	▼	:	×	✓	f_x	

◢	A	B	C	D
1				
2		June 30, 2023		
3		6/30/2023		
4		Jun-23		
5		2023-06-30		
6		6/30/23 1:00 PM		
7		1:30 PM		
8				
9				

1.11 Excel recognizes dates and times typed using these and other formats.

If you use a format that Excel does not recognize as a date or time, Excel will either display an error or treat the entry as text (left aligned) rather than a date (right aligned). In other cases, Excel might recognize a date or time you enter but convert it to another format when you finish the entry, based on location settings for dates and times in Excel and other default date settings in the Windows operating system. Don't worry, though. Chapter 5 explains how to change the number formatting manually for dates and other numbers in the section called "Changing the Number or Date Format."

Number formatting on the fly

You've just seen how Excel can interpret date entries in cells and adjust the formatting. Similarly, Excel can recognize certain types of number formatting depending on what other characters you include with the number. Knowing how this "on the fly" formatting works can save you some typing time, as in these cases:

- **Decimals.** If you type a . (decimal point) when entering a number followed by additional numbers, that sets the number of decimal places displayed in the cell. So, if you type 11.1234, Excel displays the entry with all four decimal places. However, if the last number entered after the decimal place is a 0 (zero), Excel truncates that digit. That is, 11.1230 would be displayed as 11.123.

- **Thousands (and beyond).** By default, if you type 1000 in a cell, Excel displays it as 1000. But if you include the thousands separator and enter 1,000, Excel displays it as 1,000. If you enter 1,000,000, Excel displays 1,000,000. You get the drift.

- **Currency.** You can type a currency symbol such as the $ (dollar sign) or € (Euro symbol) at the beginning of an entry, and Excel will recognize it as currency. Include a decimal point and two decimal places, and comma separators if needed, as well.

- **Percentages.** Now, this is where things get a little trickier because of how percentages work in math. A percentage is part of the whole. In math, the "whole" value is 1.00 or 100%. So .25 is 25%, .75 is 75%, and so on. Years ago in Excel, you had to enter the decimal value (such as .25) in the cell and then apply a number format to change it to a percentage. Now, you can just include the % (percent sign) when you type the value in the cell, and Excel automatically interprets it as a percentage. However, in formulas referencing the cell holding the percentage, Excel uses the corresponding decimal value to make the calculation.

Figure 1.12 shows some dates entered in column B, some values with two decimal places included in column D, and some discount amounts entered with the % (percent sign) in column E.

E14	▾	⋮	× ✓	f_x	10%	
	A	B	C	D	E	F
1	Order Summary					
2	Operator:	name@example.com				
3						
4	Order #	Date	Customer	Total	Disc. %	
5	1	6/20/2023	Ryan	99.99	15%	
6	2	6/20/2023	Miller	129.99	10%	
7	3	6/24/2023	Smith	80.95	10%	
8	4	6/28/2023	Acton	65.25	5%	
9	5	6/29/2023	Ryan	349.58	15%	
10	6	6/29/2023	Casper	79.99	5%	
11	7	6/30/2023	Smith	58.75	10%	
12	8	6/30/2023	Phillips	275.89	5%	
13	9	6/30/2023	Yelton	105.75	5%	
14	10	7/1/2023	Miller	79.99	10%	
15						

1.12 The way you type some number entries helps Excel apply a number format automatically.

Caution When a number format has been applied to a cell, even by typing as just described, the cell keeps that number format even if you later delete the cell contents. This may lead to unexpected results if you need to type a number that needs a different format later, so you'd need to clear the cell formatting or apply another number format as described in Chapter 5.

Making Selections

You've already seen how to move around the worksheet to a new active cell so that you can make a cell entry. For other operations, such as when you want to copy or move data or work with data formatting and layout, you will usually need to make larger selections. Let's run through how to do that next.

Understanding cells and ranges

A *cell* is formed by the intersection of a single worksheet row and column. A *range* encompasses a rectangular group of cells, such as multiple cells holding sales data down a column or across a row. A range also can include multiple columns or rows of information. The *address* or *reference* for a range includes the address for its upper-left cell, a : (colon), and the address for its lower-right cell, as in F10:H25. If you refer to Figure 1.12, the range D5:D14 holds the Total amount for each order. The range A7:E7 holds the information for Order 3. And the range A4:E14 holds all the order information, including the labels or headers identifying each column of data.

Selecting a range

Most users prefer to use a mouse to make selections. Just drag diagonally over the range to select it. The bold selection border or cell selector expands accordingly, and shading appears over all the cells within the border. Alternately, you can click the upper-left cell, and then Shift+click the lower-right cell. Figure 1.13 shows an example, with the range of order information selected.

A4	▼	:	×	✓	*fx*	Order #	
◢	A	B	C	D	E	F	
1	Order Summary						
2	Operator:	name@example.com					
3							
4	Order #	Date	Customer	Total	Disc. %		
5	1	6/20/2023	Ryan	99.99	15%		
6	2	6/20/2023	Miller	129.99	10%		
7	3	6/24/2023	Smith	80.95	10%		
8	4	6/28/2023	Acton	65.25	5%		
9	5	6/29/2023	Ryan	349.58	15%		
10	6	6/29/2023	Casper	79.99	5%		
11	7	6/30/2023	Smith	58.75	10%		
12	8	6/30/2023	Phillips	275.89	5%		
13	9	6/30/2023	Yelton	105.75	5%		
14	10	7/1/2023	Miller	79.99	10%		
15							

1.13 Range A4:E14 is selected.

Caution

This brings up one of my biggest tech writing pet peeves. Some tech content uses the term "click and drag" rather than just drag. By definition "click" means to press and release the mouse button, while "drag" means to press and hold the mouse button while moving the mouse, so a "click and drag" action isn't really possible. To make selections, just drag, please.

If you're out in the field with your laptop, you may not have a mouse with you and may be stuck using the trackpad. I admit it, when it comes to making Excel range selections, I'm pretty trackpad incompetent, so I tend to switch to using keyboard shortcuts to make range selections. Using the keyboard is also more efficient when the range you need to select is wider or taller than the area that can show on-screen at once. Just select the upper-left cell for the range using the method of your choice, and then press and hold the Shift key while using the right and down arrow keys to expand the selection as needed.

If you know the range address for the range you want to select, click in the Name box, type the range address, and press Enter. For example, you could type B2:C7 in the Name box and press Enter to select the range B2:C7.

You also can select a noncontiguous selection. This is a selection that basically includes two or more ranges with space in between them, meaning they are nonadjacent. Select the first range as needed, and then press and hold the Ctrl key while dragging over an additional range or ranges to add with the mouse.

To deselect a range, click any cell on the sheet.

Selecting a row or column

You might select an entire row that contains column labels to apply identical font formatting to all the cells, or you might select an entire column when you want to adjust the column width or fill with a different background color. You also can select multiple rows or columns when needed. To select one or more rows or columns, follow these steps:

1. **Move the mouse pointer over the row or column header for the (first) row or column to select, until the mouse pointer changes to a black right arrow or down arrow.** (See Figure 1.14.)

2. **Perform one of the following actions:**

   ◉ **Click the header for the row or column to select it.**

   ◉ **Drag down to select multiple rows or right to select multiple columns.**

Select All button

Mouse pointer for selecting column

Selected column

D1	▼ :	× ✓	fx			
◢	A	B	C	D	E	F
1	Order Summary					
2	Operator:	name@example.com				
3						
4	Order #	Date	Customer	Total	Disc. %	
5	1	6/20/2023	Ryan	99.99	15%	
6	2	6/20/2023	Miller	129.99	10%	
7	3	6/24/2023	Smith	80.95	10%	
8	4	6/28/2023	Acton	65.25	5%	
9	5	6/29/2023	Ryan	349.58	15%	
10	6	6/29/2023	Casper	79.99	5%	
11	7	6/30/2023	Smith	58.75	10%	
12	8	6/30/2023	Phillips	275.89	5%	
13	9	6/30/2023	Yelton	105.75	5%	
14	10	7/1/2023	Miller	79.99	10%	
15						
16						
17						
18						
19						
20						
21						
22						

Figure 1.14 You can select one or more rows or columns.

Genius

If you want to select all cells in a worksheet, such as to adjust the formatting for all the cells, click the Select All button. It's in the upper-left corner of the sheet where the row and column headers intersect and has a triangle on it that points to the sheet cells (see Figure 1.14). You also can press Ctrl+A to select all the cells. Depending on the sheet contents, sometimes you need to press Ctrl+A twice to select absolutely every cell.

Working with Sheets

In recent versions of Excel, the default number of sheets in a new workbook file is one. Yep, one. That means if you want to expand to other sheets at all, you have to add the sheets into the workbook file. Theoretically, the number of sheets you can add and use in a given workbook file is limited only by the amount of memory in your computer. As a practical matter, unless you're a data scientist or other analyst working with a large data-set like US Census data or world weather data, a typical workbook file for you might need anywhere from a handful to a dozen sheets.

Adding, renaming, and jumping to a sheet

Fortunately, you can add a new sheet to the workbook with a single click. Just click the New Sheet button to the right of the existing sheet tab(s). The new sheet appears immediately. Excel assigns generic names (Sheet1, Sheet2, and so on) as you add sheets. Renaming sheets to use more meaningful names is a good practice, particularly if you will be sharing the workbook file with other users who need to understand what sheet holds which data. Follow these steps to rename a sheet:

1. **Right-click the sheet tab.**

2. **Choose Rename from the shortcut menu.** Instead of Steps 1 and 2, you also can double-click the sheet name to select it.

3. **Type a new name to replace the generic name or any previous name you assigned to the sheet.** Figure 1.15 shows the new sheet name I typed.

Sheet scrolling buttons   Generic sheet names

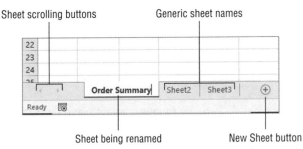

Sheet being renamed   New Sheet button

1.15 Sheets have generic numbered names until you rename them.

4. **Press Enter.**

To move from one sheet to another, click the destination sheet tab to make it the active sheet. If your workbook file has more sheets (tabs) than can display on-screen at once, the sheet scrolling (arrow) buttons to the left of the first sheet tab become active so that you can scroll the desired sheet into view using one of these techniques:

- Clicking one of the buttons scrolls one tab at a time in the direction of the button arrow.

- Ctrl+clicking either button displays the first or last sheet tab.

- Right-clicking either button opens the Activate dialog box, where you can click the name of a sheet and then click OK to display that sheet.

If you want to see more sheet tabs on-screen at a time, move the mouse pointer over the button that has three dots on it to the left of the horizontal scroll bar. When the mouse

25

pointer changes into a pair of black horizontal arrows with two vertical lines (also known as a *split pointer*), drag to the right to make more room for tabs.

Genius

You can include multiple similar sheets in a workbook file, such as if you use the same layout to collect sales information from each quarter. After you add the sheets, click the first sheet tab, and then Shift+click the last sheet tab to group the sheets. When sheets are grouped, cell entries or formatting appears in the same locations on the other grouped sheets. (This is sometimes called working with a *3-D selection*.) When finished, right-click a grouped sheet tab and choose Ungroup Sheets.

Moving or copying a sheet

You can move a sheet to change its order among the sheet tabs. Simply use the mouse to drag the sheet tab left or right. As you're dragging, the mouse pointer changes to an arrow with a sheet on it. When the little black triangle above the tabs reaches the desired new sheet location, release the mouse button. Given that moving sheets becomes more difficult if you have to scroll the sheet tabs at all, take the desired sheet order into account when planning your workbook so that you can create your sheets in a solid order from the start.

Copying a sheet presents another opportunity to save data entry and formatting time. These steps lead the way:

1. **Right-click the sheet tab of the sheet you want to copy.**

2. **Choose Move or Copy from the shortcut menu**. The Move or Copy dialog box opens.

3. **Select the Create a Copy check box near the bottom of the dialog box to check it.**

4. **In the Before Sheet list, click the name of the sheet before which Excel should insert the sheet copy, or click (Move to End).** I often use the (Move to End) choice, as shown in Figure 1.16, to build a workbook a sheet at a time.

5. **Click OK.**

Note

You can use the Move or Copy dialog box to move or copy a sheet to another open workbook file. Select the destination file from the To Book drop-down list at the top of the dialog box, and then continue with Step 3 shown previously.

26

Move or Copy ? ✕

Move selected sheets
To book:

| Order Summary.xlsx | ⌄ |

Before sheet:

Order Summary	^
Sheet2	
Sheet3	
(move to end)	
	⌄

☑ Create a copy

| OK | Cancel |

1.16 Copy a sheet to reuse the information you've entered on it.

Saving and Closing a File

You can save your file and give it a unique name any time after you create the blank file or create a new file from a template. This is your opportunity to establish an orderly system for naming files, just as you should use an orderly system for naming and organizing folders. After all, how are you going to find your work later if you can't navigate to the right folder and don't know what you named the file? For example, if you work with a variety of clients, you could create a folder for each client using File Explorer in Windows 10. Then each file for a particular client could start with a project number and include the client name and year and month, as in *0123 BestClient 2023-06.*

From there, saving a file will seem similar to the process for opening a file covered earlier in this chapter. Follow these steps:

1. **Choose File → Save As.** (You also can choose File → Save the first time you save a file.) The Save As screen that appears again gives you the option of working with recently used folders in the list at the far right or working with the other save locations listed more toward the middle. Again, I'm going to stick with the traditional method of using the Save As dialog box. Feel free to explore other methods the screen presents on your own.

2. **Toward the middle, under Other Locations, click Browse.** Because the default save location set in Word options is the Documents folder for your Windows 10 user account, the address that initially appears at the top of the Save As dialog box reads This PC > Documents >.

3. **Use the Navigation pane and file list to navigate to the folder where you want to save the file.**

4. **Edit the name in the File Name text box as desired.** Figure 1.17 shows the Save As dialog box.

1.17 Workbook files have generic numbered names until you rename them.

5. **Click Save.**

To resave a file as you periodically add data or make changes, choose File ➜ Save, click the Save button on the QAT, or press Ctrl+S. After saving the file, you can choose File ➜ Close to close the file without exiting Excel.

Another Way to Save

When you save a new file for the first time, clicking the Save button on the QAT or pressing Ctrl+S works a bit differently than the File → Save or Save As command. A Save This File window opens. You can enter a name in the File Name text box and then choose a default or recently used location from the Choose a Location drop-down list. (For at least one of my Microsoft 365 accounts, the default location listed is OneDrive in this list.) After choosing a location, click the Save button. This can be a good route for saving new files if you frequently save to the default location or one or two other folders.

How Do I Make Changes to My Sheet?

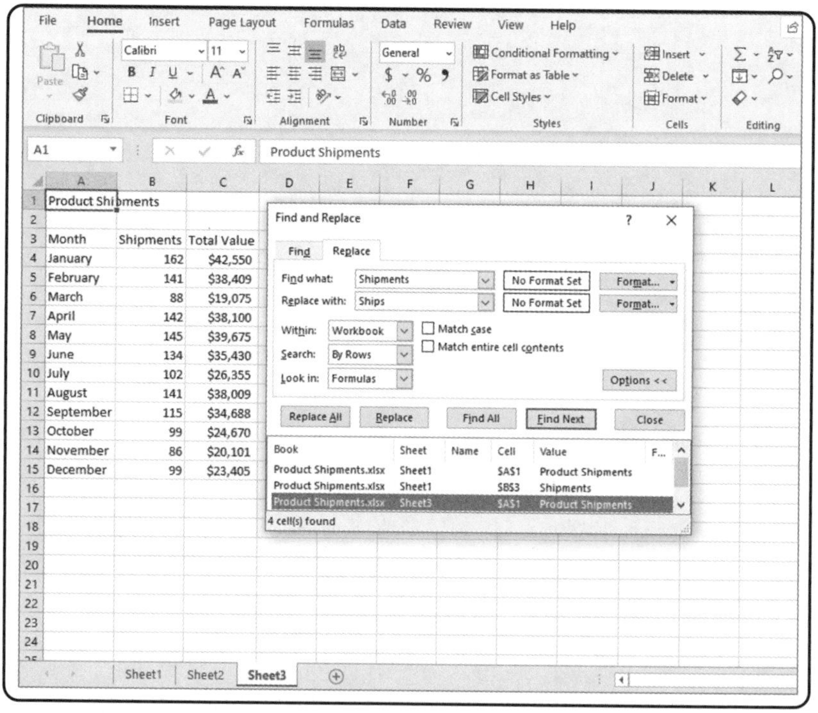

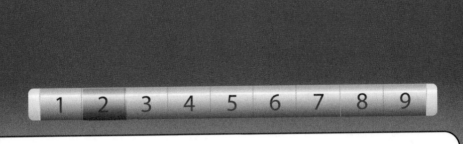

Often, your initial stab at entering information into a worksheet in an arrangement that meets your needs is really just a first draft. Some of the values may have changed since you made your initial cell entries, you may need to add some new data, or you may need to make a few adjustments to make navigating the sheet easier. Excel includes numerous tools to make updating and improving your sheets a breeze. In this chapter, I show you how to handle some of those cleanup tasks for making your Excel content more accurate and easy to use.

Cell Editing Basics

Editing the cell entries in your workbook files is another core task because, well, typos happen and the circumstances driving data change. You might identify an error in a formula that you need to correct. Or, consider a project schedule being tracked in Excel. If a team member misses a deliverable date, then the cell holding that deliverable date must be changed.

Making changes

Fortunately, changing cell contents in Excel is as easy as typing the contents in the first place. And, Excel gives you a few options for making changes:

- **Replacing a cell entry.** To replace the contents of a cell, click the cell, type the new contents, and then press Tab or Enter.

- **Editing in the cell.** Click the cell or select it using the keyboard, and then either press F2 or double-click the cell's contents to place the insertion point in the cell. Use the keyboard keys to make changes (including arrow keys to move the insertion point, and Backspace and Delete to remove characters), and then press Enter or Tab.

- **Editing in the Formula bar.** Click the cell, and then click in the cell contents in the Formula bar using the keyboard as just described for editing in the cell. You can then press Enter or Tab or click the Enter button on the Formula bar, which appears in Figure 2.1.

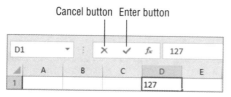

2.1 Click the Enter button on the Formula bar to finish editing a cell.

Note The Formula bar also has a Cancel button, which cancels your changes to the cell. You also can use the Cancel and Enter buttons when you're making your initial entries in cells.

Commenting when editing

If you're collaborating with others on workbook changes, you might use the comments and notes features in Excel. You might add a comment to a cell to ask a question about a value or add a note to document the source for a figure. After clicking a cell, choose Review → Comments → New Comment or Review → Notes → Notes → New Note. You also can right-click the cell and choose either New Comment or New Note. Type the comment or note in the box that appears. To finish a comment, click the Post button at the bottom of the box. To finish a note, just click outside it.

A cell with a comment has a purple comment marker in the upper-right corner, while a cell with a note has a red triangle. Move the mouse pointer over the cell to view the comment or note. You also can respond to a comment you've displayed by clicking in the Reply text box, typing your response, and then clicking the Post button at the bottom. The Comments group and Notes menu on the Review tab also have choices for moving between comments or notes.

You can delete a cell's comment with Review → Comments → Delete Comment. That command also seems to work for deleting notes. Tricky! Or, you can right-click the cell and choose Delete Note to remove the note.

Clearing cell contents

You may need to delete or clear cell contents, such as when you're rearranging information on a sheet or deciding how to organize information on a new sheet. You can clear either an individual cell or a range that you've selected. Click the cell or select it with the keyboard, or select the range of cells to clear, and then perform one of these actions:

- Press Delete, and then press Enter or Tab. Pressing Backspace also works when you're clearing a single cell.

- Right-click the selected cell or range, and then choose Clear Contents (see Figure 2.2).

- Choose Home → Editing → Clear → Clear Contents.

Caution

Clearing a cell's contents doesn't clear the formatting applied, and in the case of number formats, this can cause surprises if you need to make an entry in the cell later. The Home → Editing → Clear menu also has Clear Formats and Clear All choices for clearing more than just the cell contents.

B3		⋮		X	Cut			
				[]	Copy		F	G
▲	A	B		[]	**Paste Options:**			
1	Product Shipment							
2					[]			
3	Month	Dollars			Paste Special...			
4								
5				℗	Smart Lookup			
6								
7					Insert...			
8					Delete...			
9								
10					Clear Contents			
11								
12					Translate			
13								
14					Quick Analysis			
15					Filter	>		
16								
17					Sort	>		
18					Get Data from Table/Range...			
19								
20					New Comment			
21					New Note			
22								
23					Format Cells...			
24					Pick From Drop-down List...			

2.2 You can use a shortcut menu to clear the contents from a cell.

Using Undo and Redo

As you begin to make changes in your sheet, you may have the occasional "Darn! I didn't mean to do that" moment. Lucky for you, Excel has Undo! When you've made a change that you decide you don't want, click the Undo button (with the left-swooping arrow) on the QAT or press Ctrl+Z. After you've undone at least one action, the button for Undo's pal Redo also becomes active on the QAT. You can click it or press Ctrl+Y to redo the change that you just undid.

There are situations where undoing an action immediately is warranted to avoid really messing up your worksheet data. For example, if you sort a list that doesn't have a numbered column indicating the original order of the rows, you can only return the list to its original order with Undo.

Genius

Excel tracks all actions you take during the current work session, which can be dozens. If you want to backtrack and undo numerous actions, click the Undo button's drop-down list arrow, move the mouse pointer over the oldest action to undo, and then click the action. Excel undoes that action as well as all the others above it in the undo history. The Redo button's drop-down list works the same when you want to redo multiple actions that you've undone.

Spell-checking your work

You may have noticed that Excel automatically corrects some typos and formatting as you go, using its AutoCorrect and AutoFormat features. While these features do catch many common errors, you may encounter situations where you need to recheck some entries yourself or have Excel check for spelling and grammar errors for you. Follow these steps to run a spelling check:

1. **Select a single cell or a range of cells to check.** When you select a single cell, the spelling check feature checks all cells in the worksheet.

2. **Choose Review → Proofing → Spelling or press F7.** If an error is found, the Spelling dialog box opens.

3. **Click the desired fix in the Suggestions list and then click either Change or Change All.** You also can use other buttons to ignore the spelling, add the spelling to the dictionary, and more. Repeat changing and/or ignoring words that the Spelling dialog box flags as needed.

4. **If you see a message box asking whether to continue from the beginning of the sheet, click Yes.**

5. **Click OK in the message box telling you the spell-check is complete.**

Copying or Moving a Range

The ability to copy or move existing content in Excel means you don't have to retype and reformat a new range of cells. As easily as you can pick up and move a pen on your desk, you can copy or move a range from one spot to another in Excel. The method you use to make the copy or move depends somewhat on location.

◢	A	B	C	D
1	Product Shipments			
2				
3	Month	Total Value		
4				
5				
6				

2.3 Using the mouse works well when copying or moving a range within the visible sheet area.

If you just need to copy the information or move it on the current sheet within an area that's visible on-screen, drag-and-drop editing with the mouse works well. Select the cell or range to move, and then point to the selection border so that the mouse pointer changes to include a black four-headed arrow, as shown in Figure 2.3. To move the selected range, just drag it to the new location. To copy the selected range, press and hold the Ctrl key so that the mouse pointer changes again to include a small plus sign, and then drag until the copy of the range reaches the destination you want.

Moving or copying with the mouse becomes impractical for distances beyond the current screen, because Excel tends to scroll quickly or sometimes jump by a full screen at a time. And using the mouse to copy between sheets or workbook files is an obvious no go. In these scenarios, you should use the Copy, Cut, and Paste commands, as explained in these steps:

1. **Select the cell or range to copy or move.**

2. **Choose Home → Clipboard → Copy to copy the selection or Home → Clipboard → Cut to move the selection.** You use the Cut command when moving the selection because you want to remove it from its original location.

3. **Navigate to the new location for the copied or cut information, whether elsewhere on the sheet, on another sheet, or in another workbook file.**

4. **If needed, click the upper-left cell in the range where you want to place the copied or cut selection.**

5. **Choose Home → Clipboard → Paste.** Be sure to click the top part of the Paste button. The copied or cut selection appears in the new location.

Caution

When you paste, Excel will replace existing contents in the destination location. Make sure that when you click a cell in Step 4, there's a range of empty cells below and to the right that's big enough to hold the selection you made in Step 1.

Purists maintain that using a mouse to choose commands slows you down because you have to take your hand off the keyboard. In case you subscribe to that opinion, as I tend to because I type a lot, the keyboard shortcuts for the Copy, Cut, and Paste commands are Ctrl+C, Ctrl+X, and Ctrl+V. These three keyboard shortcuts work in Windows and most Windows programs. In most cases, you can click the upper-left cell of the destination range and just press Enter to paste after copying or cutting.

Genius

The Clipboard is a memory holding area that Windows uses when you copy or paste information. Microsoft 365 has an expanded Clipboard that by default holds up to 24 items that you've copied during your current work session in Excel. Click the dialog box launcher in the Clipboard group of the Home tab to open the Clipboard pane, and then double-click a copied item to insert it into the sheet at the active cell.

Using Paste Special

The Paste button in the Clipboard group of the Home tab is one of the ribbon's split buttons that I mentioned in Chapter 1. If you click the bottom half of the button with the down arrow on it after copying or cutting and selecting the upper-left cell of the destination range, the choices shown in Figure 2.4 appear. The choices enable you to control exactly what content pastes (formulas, values, or both) and whether it keeps the same formatting. You also can paste a link to the source data or paste a picture or linked picture of the original data. The Transpose choice in the Paste section at the top of the menu changes the orientation of the data when pasted. For example, if you had some data labels listed down a column, Transpose would paste them across a single row, instead, as Figure 2.4 also illustrates. To see a ScreenTip identifying a choice on the Paste menu and its keyboard shortcut, move the mouse pointer over it. Then click the button or press the keyboard shortcut for the specific type of paste you need to perform.

If you click Paste Special at the bottom of the Paste menu, the Paste Special dialog box opens (Figure 2.5). It offers even more choices than the Paste menu, notably in the Operation section. For example, if you chose the Add option there, the paste would add the values in the copied or cut selection to the existing values entered in the destination range. After you choose an option in the Paste Special dialog box, click OK to finish the paste.

Genius

After you perform a regular paste, the Paste Options button appears near the lower-right corner of the pasted range. Click it to open a menu with the same choices as the Paste menu, and then choose the type of paste to perform.

Copied labels   Pasted and transposed labels

2.4 Excel provides many different ways to paste a selection.

2.5 The Paste Special dialog box provides even more special ways to paste.

Using Auto Fill and Filling Series

While you're free to arrange and track your information any way that you want to in Excel, there are some common conventions that people generally follow. In business, it's typical to track results by the month or quarter, for instance. Excel's Auto Fill feature can automatically enter some lists of information for you, including the following:

38

- **Days of the week.** *Mon, Tue, Wed. . .* or *Monday, Tuesday, Wednesday. . .*

- **Month names.** *Jan, Feb, Mar. . .* or *January, February, March. . .*

- **Quarters.** *Q1, Q2, Q3. . .* or *Qtr1, Qtr2, Qtr3. . .*

- **Other labels with a number added.** *Week 1, Week 2, Week 3. . .* or *Quintile 1, Quintile 2, Quintile 3. . .*

Caution

For the first three types of Auto Fill lists noted here, Excel correctly restarts the list when needed after it fills the first full set of entries, such as filling *Monday* after *Sunday* or *Q1* after *Q4*. For the last numbered label type of list, it keeps incrementing the number. So even though Quintile indicates five groups, Excel mistakenly follows *Quintile 5* with *Quintile 6, Quintile 7,* and so on. Always double-check your Auto Fill entries for accuracy.

When you want to Auto Fill label entries down a column or across a row, follow these steps:

1. **Enter the first label in the desired cell and press Enter or Tab.** If you prefer, you can stop before pressing Enter or Tab and skip to Step 3, but I find I usually press Enter or Tab out of habit and have to reselect the cell anyway.

2. **Reselect the cell with the first entry.**

3. **Move the mouse pointer over the small box, called the *fill handle,* at the bottom-right corner of the cell selector until the mouse pointer changes to a small black plus.**

4. **Drag down the column or across the row to fill as many cells as needed.** Figure 2.6 shows an Auto Fill operation in progress. As you drag, a ScreenTip appears with the mouse pointer showing the entry being filled (December in this case). Check it out, and when it shows the last label you need in your list, release the mouse button to stop dragging. If you go too far before you stop dragging, simply reverse directions.

You can Auto Fill formulas, too, a subject that I cover in Chapter 3 in the section called "How referencing works when filling, copying, or moving a formula."

Genius

If Auto Fill can't fill the desired list, you can create a custom list. Choose File → Options. Click Advanced at the left side of the Excel Options dialog box, and then scroll down to the General section. Click the Edit Custom Lists button, and leave NEW LIST selected under Custom Lists. In the List Entries text box, type each text entry for the list and press Enter. Click Add to make the list, and click OK twice to close both dialog boxes.

A4	▼	:	✕	✓	*fx*	January

◢	A	B	C	D	E
1	Product Shipments				
2					
3	Month	Total Value			
4	January				
5					
6					
7					
8					
9					
10					
11					
12					
13					
14					
15					
16		December			
17					

Fill mouse pointer with ScreenTip

2.6 Use Auto Fill to enter a series of labels by dragging.

There are three ways to fill the same entry in multiple cells. I've never had a need to do that, but in case you do, here's how:

- Select the range, type the entry to fill, and then press Ctrl+Enter.

- To fill the same number, enter the number and use the fill handle as described previously.

- Enter the label or value, select the range to fill, and then choose Home ➔ Editing ➔ Fill ➔ Down or Home ➔ Editing ➔ Fill ➔ Right.

If you caught it in that second bullet, the fill handle by default just repeats a numeric entry if you fill it. That seems counterintuitive, but it makes sense because as you saw with filling labels, Excel has to know what pattern it's repeating. A single numeric entry can't form a pattern, so you have to make and select at least two numeric entries to establish the pattern or increment between values. For example, if you entered 1 and 1.25, selected the two cells holding those entries, and then dragged the fill handle, Excel would fill *1.5, 1.75, 2*, and so on, based on the .25 increment between the first two values.

The fancy name for this activity is filling a series of numbers. By default, the filled series is a *linear* trend, meaning the fill assumes the same increment, or step value, between each of the entries you select as the basis for the fill. Excel adds the step value to each item in the series to determine the next value. If you enter and select more than two values and the increments aren't the same, you won't get the fill results you expected, and it may be a little tough to interpret the results.

Showing Growth with a Series Fill

You can fill a growth series or trend rather than a linear series. Growth trends can be handy when you're trying to make business or economic forecasts, among other uses. In a growth series, Excel multiplies each value by the step value to determine the next value. For example, if you entered 1 and 5 in two cells and then selected those cells and filled a growth series, the next entries would be *25, 125, 625, 3125,* and so on, generating larger numbers fairly quickly. That's because the first two entries, 1 and 5, established that each subsequent value should be multiplied by 5. One way to fill a growth series is to enter the first two values, select the range to fill (including the first two entries you made in the selection) down the row or across the column, and then choose Home ➜ Editing ➜ Fill ➜ Series. In the Series dialog box that appears, click Growth under Type and click the Trend check box to check it. Click OK. The even easier way to fill a growth series—and I just learned this doozy of a tip myself—is to enter and select the first two values and then right-drag with the mouse. (Right-dragging means to press and hold the right mouse button rather than the left mouse button while dragging.) In the shortcut menu that appears, choose Growth Trend.

Inserting and Deleting Rows, Columns, and Cells

You can change the layout of your worksheets as needed when your reporting and communications needs change. For example, your boss might ask you to include a column for another metric in a sheet you've already created. Or, if a colleague provides you a workbook file with data exported from another source such as your company's inventory database, you might need to delete the rows or columns with information that's not pertinent to your team's decision-making.

You can insert and delete one or more cells, rows, or columns as needed. Working with rows and columns is easiest, and there are a couple of different techniques you can use to get the job done:

● **Right-click the header for a single row or column in the location where you want to insert or delete, and choose Insert or Delete in the shortcut menu, which is shown in Figure 2.7.**

2.7 Right-click a row or column header, and then click Insert or Delete.

● **Select multiple rows or columns in the desired location, and then right-click and choose Insert or Delete.** Or, rather than using the shortcut menu, you can choose Home ➜ Cells ➜ Insert or Home ➜ Cells ➜ Delete.

Note

The Home ➜ Cells ➜ Insert and Home ➜ Cells ➜ Delete buttons each have a drop-down arrow that you can click to open a menu with additional choices, but that's often not necessary when inserting and deleting rows and columns as just described.

When you insert one or more new rows, the rows below shift down. When you insert one or more new columns, the columns to the right shift further right. When you delete rows or columns, the opposite happens: rows below shift up, and columns to the right shift left.

Caution Excel doesn't give you any warning when you're deleting rows and columns, so check carefully when you're deleting rows and columns and remember to use your friend, Undo, if needed.

Inserting or deleting a range of cells takes a little more thought, as Excel asks you to choose how it should shift information on the worksheet. To insert or delete a range, follow these steps:

1. **Select the range where you want to insert or delete cells.**

2. **Right-click the selection and click Insert or Delete.** The Insert or Delete dialog box appears, prompting you to specify how to shift the cells. Figure 2.8 shows the Delete dialog box. The Insert dialog box looks similar.

3. **Click the option button for the way you want the data to shift.** For example, when deleting, Shift Cells Left will move all the cells on the same rows as the selection to the left to replace the deleted data, while Shift Cells Up will move all the cells in the same columns as the selection up to replace the deleted data. When you're inserting data, the Insert dialog box has Shift Cells Right and Shift Cells Down choices.

2.8 Excel prompts you to specify how it should shift cells when you're inserting or deleting a range.

4. **Click OK to finish and close the dialog box.**

If you choose the Home → Cells → Insert or Home → Cells → Delete button directly when inserting or deleting a range, Excel doesn't display a dialog box. It immediately inserts or deletes the cells, shifting the other cells on the same row as the selection to the right when inserting or left when deleting.

43

Genius

You can hide rows or columns holding sensitive data. First select the rows or columns. Then right-click the selection and choose Hide. To redisplay the hidden rows or columns, select the rows above and below the hidden area or the columns to the left and right of the hidden area. Right-click the selection and choose Unhide. The Home → Cells → Format → Hide & Unhide submenu also has choices for hiding and unhiding rows, columns, and sheets.

Creating Range Names

In Excel, you can assign a range name to any range, even a one-cell range. Why would you want to take the time to do this? Convenience, plain and simple. When a range has a name, you can select the range quickly using the Name box at the left end of the Formula bar. And, as the Chapter 4 section titled "Using Range Names in Formulas" explains, you can use a range name rather than a range address in some formulas. Descriptive range names make working in the file more user friendly.

Range names can be up to 255 characters long, but within that broad guideline, there are some additional rules you have to follow. Short, descriptive names are the best, and you generally cannot duplicate the same name within the workbook file. The range name can't be the same as a cell address, like C4. Range names can be a single letter, but you cannot use the letters R and C, which are used in Excel for an alternate cell reference style. The range name must start with a letter, _ (underscore), or \ (backslash), and cannot include spaces. You can use the . (period), ? (question mark), _ (underscore), and \ (backslash) symbols within the name, but not as the first character, with the exception of _ (underscore) and \ (backslash). It's common to use the _ (underscore) character rather than a space. If you happen to try to use a range name that's the same as another range name that Excel might be using, Excel may prevent you from assigning the range name.

Genius

After you assign the range name, you can reselect that range at any time by typing the name in the Name box and pressing Enter or by clicking the down arrow at the right end of the Name box and choosing the name of the range to select. Even if you capitalize range names when you create them, range names are not case sensitive. Typing the range name in all lowercase letters when using the Name box to reselect the range works.

Using the Name box

As with many of the other Excel operations you've seen so far, Excel lets you choose from a few different methods for assigning a range name. First, here are the steps to follow if you want to use the Name box to name a range:

1. **Select the range to name.** If the range you're naming contains values and has an identifying label above it or to the left, you should omit that label from your selection as a best practice. This is because including the label with the numeric values might create an error if you try to use the range name in some formulas.

2. **Click in the Name box to select its contents.**

3. **Type the range name in the Name box, as in the example in Figure 2.9.**

4. **Press Enter.**

New range name entered in Name box

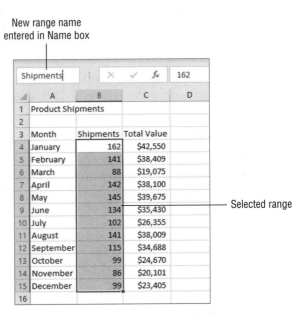

Selected range

2.9 You can create a range name using the Name box.

Note

If you make any change that shifts the position of the range you selected and named, the range retains the name you assigned, even in its new location. So if you added a column to the left of the named range, the named range just shifts one column to the right. If you add rows or columns within the named range, the range expands to encompass them, so there's no need to repeat the steps for naming the range.

Using the New Name dialog box

By default, a range you create with the Name box has a Workbook scope assigned, meaning it can be used throughout the workbook file. That is, if the named range is on Sheet1 and you want to reference the range in a formula in a cell on Sheet2, you could. In other cases, you might want to limit the use of a range name within the sheet holding the named range. You might create a range with a scope limited to the current sheet if you want to use the same range name on multiple sheets within the workbook file.

The New Name dialog box enables you to assign a scope when naming a range. To create a range name using the New Name dialog box, follow these steps:

1. **Select the range to name.** Again, it is advisable to not include any label in the range of values.

2. **Choose Formulas → Defined Names → Define Name.** The New Name dialog box appears. As shown in Figure 2.10, Excel may suggest a range name for you in the Name text box, basing that name on the label beside or above the selected range.

2.10 The New Name dialog box enables you to choose the scope for a new range name.

3. **Edit any suggested name in the Name text box as desired.**

4. **Open the Scope drop-down list and click the name of a sheet to limit the scope of the new range name to that sheet.** Of course, this step is optional, as is making an entry in the Comment text box.

5. **Click OK.**

Assigning multiple range names at once

You might typically enter the numerical data you want to calculate in Excel in a nice, contiguous block, with labels down the column at the left and a row with labels above the data. If your data is in an arrangement like this, chances are Excel's Create from Selection command can create names for all the ranges for you. To try this shortcut, follow these steps:

Genius

This is my new favorite selection keyboard shortcut: click any cell in a contiguous range to select and press Ctrl+Shift+*. Excel selects the whole area. Ctrl+A also selects a contiguous range when you've selected a cell in the range or, as covered in Chapter 1, the whole sheet when a cell outside a contiguous range is selected.

1. **Select the larger range of data that holds all the smaller ranges you want to name.**

2. **Choose Formulas → Defined Names → Create from Selection or press Ctrl+Shift+F3.** The Create Names from Selection dialog box opens.

3. **Clear or check boxes as needed to specify which cells hold the labels to use for the range names.** For example, in Figure 2.11, I cleared the check beside Left Column because I only wanted to create names for the ranges in the selected columns.

4. **Click OK.** This operation assigned three range names in my example workbook file: Month, Shipments, and Total_Value.

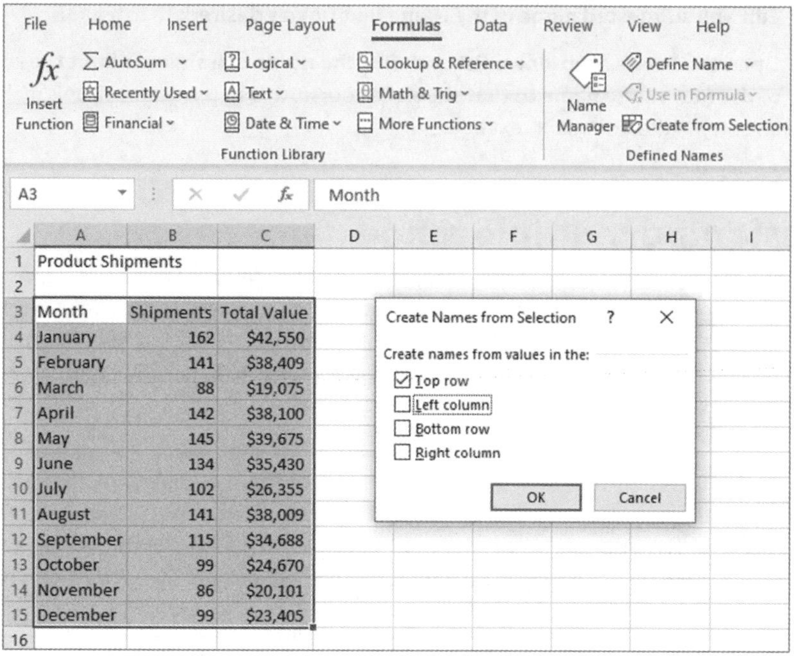

| | File | Home | Insert | Page Layout | | Formulas | Data | Review | View | Help |

2.11 The Create from Selection command opens this dialog box for assigning multiple range names at once.

Deleting a range name

You don't have to keep the range names you've assigned in a workbook file. You can delete a name if it becomes obsolete. For example, because the Month range shown in Figure 2.11 doesn't hold any values and the only reason I'd likely need to select it again would be to change its formatting, I might delete the Month range name assigned to it when I used the Formulas → Defined Names → Create From Selection command.

To use the Name Manager dialog box to delete a range name, follow these steps:

1. **Choose Formulas → Defined Names → Name Manager or press Ctrl+F3.**

2. **In the list of range names (Figure 2.12), click the range name to delete, if needed.**

3. **Click the Delete button above the list.** A message box asks you to confirm the deletion.

4. **Click OK.**

5. **Click Close to close the Name Manager dialog box.**

2.12 Deleting a range name removes it from the workbook file.

Caution Click the Edit button in the Name Manager dialog box to open the Edit Name dialog box. However, in that dialog box, you are limited to change the name and the range that the range name refers to. You cannot change the scope of the range. If you need to change the scope, first delete the range, and then re-create it using the Formulas ➔ Defined Names ➔ Define Name command and the resulting New Name dialog box.

49

Using Find and Replace

You might need to change entries throughout a workbook file, such as when you learn you've misspelled a product name. In a case like this, the Find and Replace dialog box is your friend. You've probably performed a find and replace operation in another program such as a word processing program, so here's a refresher of the basic steps to run through a find or replace in Excel:

1. **Choose Home → Editing → Find & Select → Find or Home → Editing → Find & Select → Replace.**

2. **Enter the word, phrase, or value to find in the Find What text box, and if replacing, enter the replacement information in the Replace With text box.**

3. **Use the Find Next or Replace buttons to review or replace entries one by one.**

4. **Click Close.**

Pretty standard, right? Even so, I want to explore a few choices you can use to accelerate or refine your find and replace operations:

- **Keyboard shortcuts.** Ctrl+F opens the Find and Replace dialog box to the Find tab, while Ctrl+H opens the dialog box with the Replace tab displayed.

- **Options.** Clicking the Options button displays numerous additional choices for refining your search, such as including formatting, matching case, or the matching the entire cell entry; controlling whether to search within the whole workbook or current sheet; and more. Clicking the Options button again hides the options.

- **Replace All.** If you're working on the Replace tab and click Replace All, Excel immediately replaces all the matches it finds and displays a message box informing you how many replacements were made. Click OK to close this dialog box. Just be sure that every time you use this button, you check the Find What and Replace With entries carefully to avoid unwanted errors. If a bad replacement happens, close the Find and Replace dialog box and click Undo on the QAT pronto.

- **Find All.** This is an interesting choice on both the Find and Replace tabs that lets you skip the match-by-match review process, if desired. It works especially well when there might be a lot of matches but you have an idea of what sheet a match you want to change might be on. After you click the Find All button, the list of matches appears at the bottom of the Find and Replace dialog box, as shown in

Figure 2.13. Clicking a match displays the sheet holding the match and selects the cell with the match behind the Find and Replace dialog box, which stays open. You can use the list to browse matches in the order that you prefer.

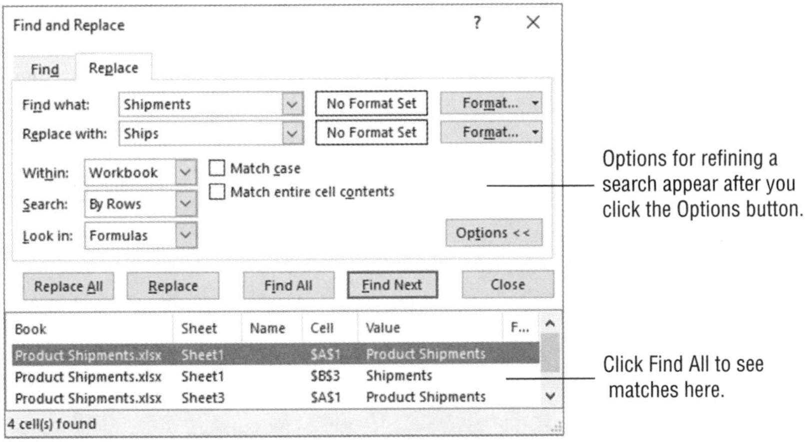

| Find and Replace | ? | X |

Options for refining a search appear after you click the Options button.

Click Find All to see matches here.

2.13 You can explore more options and shortcuts in the Find and Replace dialog box.

Genius

Most dialog boxes are modal, meaning while the dialog box is on-screen, you can only work in the dialog box. The Find and Replace dialog box, in contrast, is nonmodal or modeless. This means that while the dialog box is open, you can click in the file and make changes, such as if you see a typo after clicking the Find Next button, and then click anywhere in the dialog box to return to using it.

Freezing Rows and Columns On-Screen

Terms such as *business intelligence* (BI), *data analytics*, *data mining*, and *data visualization* have become very "buzzy" in the last several years. Generally speaking, those terms refer to using various techniques to tease meaning and insight out of very large datasets, especially for decision-making in a large organization.

You might not be working with a massive dataset, but you might have a sheet with a few dozen columns of product details or a few hundred rows of sales transactions. In those instances, it can be hard to keep the detail data in context if the important column or row label information scrolls off the screen as you move around to review and edit the data. The solution? Using the Freeze Panes choices to freeze vital row or column information (or both) on-screen, while retaining the ability to scroll around the other nonfrozen data. You have three basic Freeze Panes choices, each of which apply on the current sheet when used:

● **Freezing the top row only.** To do this, choose View ➔ Window ➔ Freeze Panes ➔ Freeze Top Row. With the top row frozen, when you scroll down, it remains on-screen.

● **Freezing the left column only.** To do this, choose View ➔ Window ➔ Freeze Panes ➔ Freeze First Column. With the left column frozen, when you scroll right, it remains on-screen.

Caution

The commands for freezing the top row or left column cannot be used together and essentially switch between each other. If you want to freeze one or more rows *and* columns, you have to use a different command. To do this, choose View ➔ Window ➔ Freeze Panes ➔ Freeze Panes.

● **Freeze one or more rows and columns.** To do this, click the cell that's both below the row(s) you want to freeze and to the right of the column(s) you want to freeze, and then choose View ➔ Window ➔ Freeze Panes ➔ Freeze Panes. For example, in the worksheet shown in Figure 2.14, I clicked cell B13 before choosing View ➔ Window ➔ Freeze Panes ➔ Freeze Panes, which froze rows 1 through 12 and column A on-screen. Notice that I've scrolled down and right so that row 109 displays below row 12 and column G appears to the right of column A. Slightly darker gridlines also identify the frozen panes.

To unfreeze panes, choose View ➔ Window ➔ Freeze Panes ➔ Unfreeze Panes.

Columns jump from A to G
because column A is frozen.

	A	G	H	I
1	U.S. Energy Information Administration			
2	June 2020 Monthly Energy Review			
3				
4	Note: Information about data precision.			
5				
6	Release Date: June 25, 2020			
7	Next Update: July 28, 2020			
8				
9	Table 1.1 Primary Energy Overview			
10				
11	Month	Primary Energy Exports	Primary Energy Net Imports	Primary Energy Stock Change and O
12		(Quadrillion Btu)	(Quadrillion Btu)	(Quadrillion Btu)
109	1981 January	0.260909	1.066928	
110	1981 February	0.276662	0.916391	
111	1981 March	0.369183	0.804578	
112	1981 April	0.324137	0.742355	
113	1981 May	0.273023	0.839534	
114	1981 June	0.245397	0.776954	
115	1981 July	0.392644	0.728799	
116	1981 August	0.41954	0.694033	
117	1981 September	0.410856	0.772868	
118	1981 October	0.465502	0.694912	
119	1981 November	0.439771	0.650898	
120	1981 December	0.429619	0.723536	

Rows jump from 12 to 109
because rows 1 through 12
are frozen.

Slightly darker gridlines
identify the frozen panes.

2.14 Rows 1 through 12 and column A are frozen on-screen in this sheet.
Source: U.S. Energy Information Administration (July 2020).

How Do I Add Up the Numbers with Formulas?

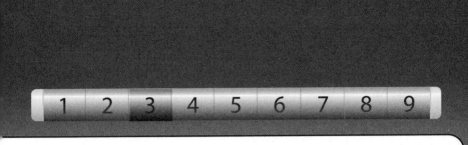

Mainframe computers from the 1970s were costly, filled a whole room, and had a fraction of the processing power of today's typical home or business computer. And with sophisticated software like Excel installed, your computer gains the capability of performing hundreds or thousands of complicated calculations—once you've set those computations up, that is. This chapter introduces you to creating formulas in Excel. It covers not only how to enter a formula, but also how to use operators correctly and otherwise structure the formula to calculate correctly, how to work with the different types of cell references, and how to look out for errors.

Entering a Basic Formula

A formula is a special type of cell entry that performs a calculation or produces another result. You can almost think of a formula as a tiny little computer program that (usually) does one specific thing. Many formulas calculate numeric values, but formulas can do other things, such as return a text result or tell you whether a condition is true or false. Building formulas can become a complex topic, so this book actually has two chapters introducing the topic. This chapter starts with the rough mechanics of entering and structuring a formula.

Typing the formula

On its face, typing a formula into a cell works like making any other cell entry: select the cell, type the contents, and press Enter or Tab. However, when you enter a formula, you have to follow structural and mathematical rules for creating the formula correctly so that it can produce the desired result, with accuracy.

The first rule: a formula must begin with an = (equal) sign. If you leave off the = (equal) sign, Excel will treat the entry like text or a value, instead.

From there, a formula generally includes one or more of these parts:

- **Constants.** These are numbers and text entered in the formula, such as the number 10.

- **Cell or range references.** When you use a reference to a cell or range, Excel uses the contents of that cell or range, usually values, in the formula's calculation. You can type the cell and range references using lowercase letters, if you prefer, and Excel will change the references to uppercase letters.

- **Operators.** These are the symbols that tell Excel what type of calculation to perform, such as + (plus) for addition and - (minus) for subtraction. A later section covers the operators you can use in formulas.

- **Functions.** Functions are essentially shortcuts for building more complex formulas without having to figure out all of the underlying math on your own. Chapter 4 covers functions.

After you finish entering a formula, its result appears in the cell rather than the formula itself. If you select a cell holding a formula, the formula appears in the Formula bar. You can edit a formula using any of the same three methods as for other cell entries: double-clicking in the cell, pressing F2, or using the Formula bar.

Cell and range references in formulas

Figure 3.1 shows a few examples of basic formulas using constants, cell references, and operators. Most of us start out creating easy formulas like these and gradually increase the complexity of the formulas we build. You can imagine the endless possibilities.

	A14		×	✓	fx			
	A	B	C	D	E	F	G	H
1		Values	Formula Results	Formula Entered in Column C	Calculation Performed by Formula			
2				25 =20+5	Constants 20 and 5 added			
3								
4		5		40 =B4+B6+B8	Values in cells B4, B6, and B8 added			
5		7						
6		12	3.2857143 =B8/B5		Value in cell B8 divided by value in cell B5			
7		19						
8		23		115 =B4*B8	Value in cell B4 multipled by value in cell B8			
9								

3.1 You can start with creating basic formulas like these with constants, cell references, and operators.

While in many cases it's acceptable to use constants in a formula, as in the example in cell C2 in Figure 3.1, using a cell or range reference ensures that your workbook will be more adaptable. Looking again at the examples in Figure 3.1: if you changed the entry in cell B8, the formula results in cells C4, C6, and C8 would change, because the formulas in all three of those cells contain a reference to cell B8. For most users, there might be few instances where it's best to include a constant in a formula.

The examples in Figure 3.1 don't include any range references. That's because when a range reference is used in a basic math formula, it can both create unexpected behavior where results spill into other cells and generate an error message. Range references come into play when you include functions in formulas, a topic covered in Chapter 4.

Genius

You also can create a reference to a cell or range on another sheet, commonly called a 3-D reference. Include the sheet name followed by an ! (exclamation point) before the reference, as in Sheet2!B18. If the cell or range is in another workbook file, the reference looks like this: '[Product Shipments.xlsx] Sheet2'!B18, with square brackets around the file name and single quotes before the first square bracket and the ! (exclamation point).

Using the mouse to save time

Rather than typing in cell references (or range references when you later start working with functions), you can use the mouse to select a cell (or range) to reference while creating a formula. I tend to prefer using the mouse, because it helps me avoid cell and range reference typos in my formulas.

When you are entering or editing a formula, Excel uses color coding to help you match up each reference on the sheet with the reference in the formula, either in the cell when creating the formula or in the Formula bar when editing the formula. I find this color coding to be particularly helpful when I use my mouse to build a formula, because it gives a visual confirmation that I'm selecting the correct cell or range.

Let's take a look at an example of using the mouse to create a formula in Figure 3.2. To start, I clicked cell D4 and typed the = (equal) sign. I then clicked cell B4 to enter its cell reference into the formula, typed the - (minus) sign, and clicked cell C4 to enter its cell reference into the formula. As indicated by the callouts in Figure 3.2 (because the color-coding can't appear in the grayscale imagery in this book), cell B4's selection border and shading and its matching cell reference in the formula were color coded blue while I was building the formula. Cell C4's selection border and shading and matching cell reference were color coded red. To finish the formula, I pressed Enter.

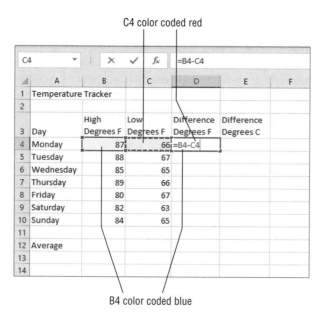

3.2 You can click a cell with the mouse to enter the cell reference in the formula.

If you were entering a range reference in a formula (as noted, almost always a formula using a function), you would drag to select the range. If the cell or range to select is on another sheet in the workbook file or in another workbook file altogether, follow these steps to use the mouse to enter the reference in the formula:

1. **If the cell or range to reference is in another workbook file, make sure both files are open.** The file where you want to enter the formula must be the current or active file.

2. **On the desired sheet, click the cell where you want to enter the formula and type the = (equal) sign.**

3. **If needed, enter any initial parts of the formula, such as a function name or open parenthesis.** A later section called "Using parentheses in formulas" details how and when to use parentheses.

4. **When you get to the point where you need to use the mouse to enter the reference, click the tab for the other sheet; or point to the Excel button on the Windows taskbar, click the thumbnail for the other file, and click the desired sheet tab.**

5. **Select the desired cell or range.**

6. **To continue the formula, type the next operator or formula part.**

7. **From there you can type other references and formula parts as needed, or repeat Steps 4 through 6 to continue using the mouse along with the keyboard to build the formula.**

8. **To finish the formula, type any remaining references or parts such as a closing parenthesis, and press Enter.**

You can use the mouse to see some quick calculations without even entering a formula. Just select a range of values, and check the status bar area to the left of the view buttons. By default, Excel shows an Average, Count, and Sum of the selected values, as shown in the example in Figure 3.3. I use this feature when I don't need to add a formula but am curious about the result of a particular calculation.

Genius

You can right-click the status bar and use the shortcut menu that appears to customize its offerings, including the calculations it displays for a selected range of values. The calculation choices are grouped near the bottom of the shortcut menu.

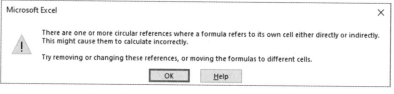

| Average: 85 | Count: 7 | Sum: 595 | | | | — | | + | 100% |

3.3 Select a range of values and then check the status bar to see Average, Count, and Sum calculations.

Dealing with minor errors

Even when you use the mouse to increase accuracy when selecting references for a formula, you can still inadvertently click the wrong cell. Or, if you're trying to create a formula that generates an error or haven't properly entered the elements of a formula, Excel displays a message box. Figure 3.4 shows an example of the former. I entered a formula with a reference to the cell where I entered it, which is a no-no because a cell can't use its own result in its formula calculation, and so on, and so on, and…. The message box in the figure is prompting me to click OK and fix the error myself or to click the Help button to learn more about the error and how to correct it.

Microsoft Excel ⊗

⚠ There are one or more circular references where a formula refers to its own cell either directly or indirectly. This might cause them to calculate incorrectly.

Try removing or changing these references, or moving the formulas to different cells.

OK Help

3.4 In some cases, Excel displays a message box prompting you to correct a formula error.

Other similar message boxes may suggest formula corrections or offer to fix the formula for you. The last section of this chapter, "Using Other Formula Review Techniques," covers how to deal with error messages that display in cells in place of the formula results.

Learning More About Operators

As you learned earlier or maybe already knew, operators are the symbols that tell Excel what type of calculation to perform. Excel enables you to use a specific subset of the available universe of mathematical operators and symbols. There are four types or categories of operators in Excel:

- **Arithmetic.** These operators perform the types of basic math you learned in school, a couple of examples of which you've already seen in this chapter.

- **Comparison.** These operators compare two values. The result is either TRUE or FALSE, which seems limited, but these operators are typically used as part of a more complex formula.

- **Concatenation.** This operator, normally used with text, enables you to combine one or more entries or contents to display a longer string of text in a cell. You would use a cell reference in the formula to refer to a cell holding text as needed. One trick to keep in mind is that you often have to create spaces manually by including " " (quote space quote) among the parts being concatenated in the formula.

- **Reference.** These operators enable you to build normal and special range references.

Table 3.1 introduces the arithmetic, comparison, and concatenation operators that you can use in Excel, along with a brief example of each. The reference operators require wordier explanations, so I cover them right after the table.

Table 3.1 Arithmetic, Comparison, and Text Operators for Excel Formulas

Type	Operator	Action/ Meaning/Use	Example	Result
Arithmetic	+	Addition	=20+5	25
Arithmetic	–	Subtraction	=20–5	15
		Negation	=–5	–5
Arithmetic	*	Multiplication	=20*5	100
Arithmetic	/	Division	=20/5	4
Arithmetic	%	Percent	=15%	.15 when used in calculation
Arithmetic	^	Exponentiation	=2^3	8
Comparison	=	Equal to	=D2=C2	TRUE when both cells contain the same value
Comparison	>	Greater than	=D2>C2	TRUE when value in cell D2 is higher
Comparison	<	Less than	=D2<C2	TRUE when value in D2 is lower
Comparison	>=	Greater than or equal to	=C10>=D10	TRUE when value in C10 is equal or higher
Comparison	<=	Less than or equal to	=C10<=D10	TRUE when value in C10 is equal or lower

Type	Operator	Action/Meaning/Use	Example	Result
Comparison	<>	Not equal to	=C10<>D10	TRUE when the values in the cells are not equal
Text	&	Concatenation	="Size"&" "&"L"	Size L

Genius

Entering the four most common operators gives the 10-key keypad another chance to shine. It includes the / (division), * (multiplication), - (subtraction), and + (addition) keys for easier formula entry. If you're a heavy Excel user and your laptop doesn't have a 10-key numeric keypad, you can get a USB version for 20 bucks or so.

The fourth category of operators, reference, holds operators that are generally used with formulas using functions, which Chapter 4 covers. The reference operators include:

- **: (colon).** You've already met this operator, used to indicate a regular range address, as in =SUM(J5:J9).

- **, (comma).** When you need to refer to multiple references, separate them with a , (comma), as in =SUM(C2:C4,F5:F7). The , (comma) is also called the union operator.

- **(space).** When you need a formula to use the contents of one or more cells located where two ranges overlap, separate the ranges with a (space), as in =SUM(D5:E10 E9:F14). This operator also can be used to generate an array. The (space) is called the intersection operator.

- **# (pound) and @ (at).** These two range operators are not typically ones the user enters. They may be used when Excel generates an array based on a formula or when you're working with an Excel table, as Chapter 7 covers. In addition, you may see the # (pound) sign used in other contexts, as when a cell holding a formula displays an error message, which is in part why I personally don't even think of them as operators.

Note

Excel enables you to insert a complex equation on a sheet for illustration purposes. You might need to do this when reporting on scientific data, for example. To insert a predefined equation, choose Insert → Symbols, and then click the bottom down arrow portion of the Equation button to display the available equations. To build your own equation, choose Insert → Symbols, and then click the top part of the Equation button. Use the Equation tab that appears to create or edit an equation.

Understanding Order of Precedence

The old saying in programming of "garbage in, garbage out," refers to the fact that if program code uses a wrong value or an improper sequence, the program will output inaccurate results, throw an error message, or not run at all. The same applies to Excel formulas. You have to be careful to reference the correct cells and use the correct constants, and you also have to be careful about the sequence and structure of the calculation. Order of precedence is one key to calculation sequence and structure.

How order of precedence works

Excel generally proceeds from the = (equal) sign to the right in evaluating a formula. For simple formulas such as the ones shown in Figures 3.1 and 3.2, this means that Excel calculates the formula from left to right, as you'd expect. But the different types of operators put a spin on the calculation order.

To determine the order of calculation in a formula, Excel follows the order of precedence, also called the *order of operations*. This means that in a longer formula with different types of operators, Excel calculates the formula in order by operator type. It only goes back to left-to-right order when two operators are at the same level or precedence. Table 3.2 lists the operators by order of precedence, from the first operations performed at the top of the table through the last performed at the bottom of the table.

Table 3.2 Order of Precedence in Excel Formulas

Order of Precedence from First to Last	Operator(s)
Reference operators	: (colon)
	(single space)
	, (comma)
Negation	– (minus), as in -1
Percent	%

Order of Precedence from First to Last	Operator(s)
Exponentiation	^
Multiplication and division	* and /
Addition and subtraction	+ and −
Concatenation	&
Comparison	=
	< >
	<=
	>=
	<
	>

You can see the order of precedence in action by considering a few simple examples with constants:

- **=10+20*5.** If this formula evaluated from left to right, the result would be 150, but because multiplication is performed before addition according to the order of precedence, the formula multiples 20*5 first, then adds 10, for a result of 110.

- **=10^2-5.** This formula calculates a result of 95, because the order of precedence says to handle exponentiation first (10 to the power of 2 is 100) and then subtraction (100-5).

- **=5+20/5-10.** If evaluated from left to right, the result would be -5 (5+20 =25, 25/5=5, 5-10=-5), but under order of precedence, 20/5 is performed first, effectively resulting in 5+4=9, 9-10=-1.

If these simple examples produce such dramatic differences, then you can imagine the massive discrepancies that could result from failure to consider the order of precedence when building a formula. Next, learn about how you can take more control of the order of calculation in a formula.

Using parentheses in formulas

I've never seen the parentheses called math operators in Excel, but I would say that they work along with the other operators to determine the result of a formula's calculation. You can use pairs of parentheses to group calculations within a formula, overriding the order of precedence. For starters, Excel calculates what's inside a pair of parentheses first. (And the parentheses must be used in pairs.) Let's look at one of the examples I listed a moment ago: =10^2-5 calculates to a result of 95. But what if I changed the formula to

=10^(2-5)? In the revised formula, Excel performs the 2-5 subtraction first, because it's in the parentheses, and then uses the result of -3 as the exponent. The revised formula calculates a result of .001.

For even more complicated formulas, you may need to nest multiple sets of parentheses within the outer set of parentheses. In that case, Excel works from the innermost set of parentheses out, taking the order of precedence into consideration as needed.

In the example temperature-tracking spreadsheet in Figure 3.5, I couldn't just take the entry from cell D4 in the Difference Degrees F column and use the standard formula to convert it from Fahrenheit to Celsius, because that would give a skewed result. Instead, I had to use the formula for converting from degrees F to degrees C—which is (F-32)*5/9—for the High Degrees F and Low Degrees F entries in cells B4 and C4, respectively, and *then* subtract the low from the high. If you count carefully in the formula shown in the Formula bar in Figure 3.5, you can see that it required six pairs of parentheses and a few layers of nesting.

Formula with nested parentheses

E4	▼	⋮	✕	✓	*fx*	=((B4-32)*(5/9))-((C4-32)*(5/9))	

◢	A	B	C	D	E	F
1	Temperature Tracker					
2						
3	Day	High Degrees F	Low Degrees F	Difference Degrees F	Difference Degrees C	
4	Monday	87	66	21	11.66666667	
5	Tuesday	88	67			

3.5 Use pairs of parentheses to group calculations and override the order of precedence.

If you leave off a closing parenthesis from any pair, in most cases Excel displays a polite message about it. You can accept a proposed correction, if any, or close the window and make the correction yourself.

Genius

It never hurts to sanity check a formula against some other resource to make sure it calculates an accurate result. For example, to verify I had gotten the formula shown in Figure 3.5 correct, I used the Temperature Converter in the Windows 10 Calculator app. You can examine the formula structure in an Excel template that's similar to your sheet (which is a great way to learn more about creating formulas in general) or ask a colleague who's an Excel whiz to take a look.

Making a Cell or Range Reference Absolute Rather Than Relative

Notice in Figure 3.5 that the use of the number 32 is truly a constant, representing the difference between the freezing point in Fahrenheit versus the freezing point in Celsius (0), for conversion purposes. You do not want this value to change if you happen to copy or move the formula. Even more, you wouldn't want to put the value 32 in a cell and reference it from the formula, because you wouldn't want another user to be able to change the value.

In other cases, a formula that you intend to copy may need to refer to a particular cell, even when you copy or move the formula, but you may need to be able to change the contents of the referenced cell in the future. Common examples of this include the cell holding the interest rate in a mortgage amortization worksheet or the cell holding a mileage rate on an expense tracking worksheet. In these scenarios, you need to change the reference type in the formula.

Changing the reference type in a formula

When you just type or use the mouse to select a cell or range reference, Excel treats it as a relative (or changeable) reference by default. We'll get to what that means more specifically in a moment. In contrast, an absolute reference in a formula cannot change. And there's a third type of reference called a *mixed reference*, where only the column letter or row number is fixed.

You can change the cell reference while entering or editing the formula. After you type or use the mouse to add the reference to the formula, immediately press the F4 key. (When editing the cell or range reference in the formula, click anywhere within the reference and press F4.) This adds a dollar sign with both the column letter and row number in the reference. In the example in Figure 3.6, the $C$3 reference is an absolute reference.

Continuing to press the F4 key cycles through the rest of the referenced types: mixed with the row fixed (as in C$3), mixed with the column fixed (as in $C3), and back to a plain old relative reference (as in C3). When the reference has been set to the type you need, either continue creating or editing the formula as needed or press Enter to finish.

Absolute range references have been a rare bird in my years of using Excel, but you might have a different experience. Again, use the F4 key when entering or editing a formula to change the reference type for a range reference. An absolute reference for a range includes dollar signs for both column letters and row numbers, as in $B$6:$B$10, and a range reference can be mixed, too.

C3		▾	⋮	×	✓	f_x	=B6*$C$3	

◢	A	B	C	D	E
1	Expense Tracker				
2					
3	Mileage Rate:		$0.54		
4					
5	Date	Miles	Reimbursement		
6	1-Jun	25	=B6*$C$3		
7	4-Jun	35			
8	9-Jun	60			
9	15-Jun	22			
10	19-Jun	40			
11					

Absolute
reference

3.6 Press F4 when entering or editing a formula to change the cell or range reference type.

How referencing works when filling, copying, or moving a formula

The default relative reference type means that if you move, copy, or fill the formula containing the reference, Excel adjusts the cell reference by the corresponding number of rows or columns as needed. For example, say the formula in cell C2 is =B2+5. If you then copy the formula down to cell C3, an increment of one row, Excel adjusts the reference in the formula by one row so the formula now reads =B3+5. That may seem like no big deal, but if you need to fill a formula down a column or across the row and have the formula references change as needed for you, this saves a huge amount of formula entry work.

In Figure 3.7, the formula in cell D4 is =B4-C4. I used the fill handle to fill the formula down through row 10. As the Formula bar in the figure shows, the formula in cell D10 is =B10-C10. Excel adjusted the relative references in the formula accordingly for each row in between 4 and 10, as well.

Genius

You also can double-click the fill handle to fill the formula down the column without dragging. Whenever you use the fill handle to perform a fill, the Auto Fill Options button appears. Click it to see variations for completing the fill operation that you can choose. Review the section in Chapter 2 called "Using Auto Fill and Filling Series" for a refresher about using Auto Fill.

Compare Figure 3.8 to Figure 3.7 to see how an absolute reference works in contrast to a relative reference. The formula in cell C6 in Figure 3.6 is =B6*$C$3. After that formula gets filled through row 10, the formula in cell C10 is =B10*$C$3. The relative reference in the formula incremented, but the absolute reference to the rate in cell C3 did not.

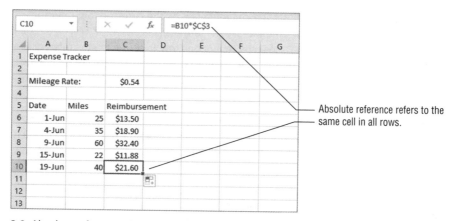

3.7 Relative references increment when a formula is filled, copied, or moved.

Relative references incremented to refer to row 10

Auto Fill Options button

Absolute reference refers to the same cell in all rows.

3.8 Absolute references do not increment when a formula is filled, copied, or moved.

And, as you might imagine, for a mixed reference, the relative row or column increments, but the fixed row or column does not when the formula is filled, copied, or moved.

Showing Formulas in Cells

I've mentioned elsewhere that examining the formulas and other elements in templates can be a great learning tool. Similarly, reviewing the formulas you've created in your own sheets can be both a learning and a troubleshooting tool. You can use this technique to refresh your memory about formulas you created in a prior workbook file, for example. Or, you can use it to check your formulas if you think you've messed up in terms of order of precedence, use of parentheses and references, or other structural issues.

To toggle between displaying formula results and formulas, choose Formulas ➔ Formula Auditing ➔ Show Formulas. As shown in Figure 3.9, the formulas immediately display in the cells. The columns temporarily change width to show all or most of each formula. In the case of Figure 3.9, I have adjusted the column widths further so that all formulas are fully visible. (If you do as I did, the column widths may also be different when you toggle formula display off, so use caution in making this type of adjustment.)

Show Formulas button

	A	B	C	D	E
1	Temperature Tracker				
2					
3	Day	High Degrees F	Low Degrees F	Difference Degrees F	Difference Degrees C
4	Monday	87	66	=B4-C4	=(((B4-32)*(5/9))-((C4-32)*(5/9)))
5	Tuesday	88	67	=B5-C5	=(((B5-32)*(5/9))-((C5-32)*(5/9)))
6	Wednesday	85	65	=B6-C6	=(((B6-32)*(5/9))-((C6-32)*(5/9)))
7	Thursday	89	66	=B7-C7	=(((B7-32)*(5/9))-((C7-32)*(5/9)))
8	Friday	80	67	=B8-C8	=(((B8-32)*(5/9))-((C8-32)*(5/9)))
9	Saturday	82	63	=B9-C9	=(((B9-32)*(5/9))-((C9-32)*(5/9)))
10	Sunday	84	65	=B10-C10	=(((B10-32)*(5/9))-((C10-32)*(5/9))
11					
12	Average	=(B4+B5+B6+B7+B8+B9+B10)/7	=(C4+C5+C6+C7+C8+C9+C10)/7	=(D4+D5+D6+D7+D8+D9+D10)/7	=(E4+E5+E6+E7+E8+E9+E10)/7
13					

3.9 Displaying workbook formulas gives you the opportunity to review your work.

Genius

You can toggle formula display on and off by pressing Ctrl plus the accent key (it's directly above the Tab key and has a tilde character on it). The un-Shifted accent character looks kind of like a short backslash, and there's not really a character to show it here. But trust me, it's there, and it works in this keyboard shortcut.

If you display formulas and print the worksheet, the formulas appear in the printout, too. This can serve as a reference tool for you, or a document you can use to train colleagues about the best practices for creating formulas in your organization. Chapter 9 covers printing in Excel.

Using Other Formula Review Techniques

The other error messages that appear in the cell start with a # (pound) sign, have all capital letters, end with a ? (question mark) or an ! (exclamation point), and appear in bold, as if to say **#ALERT!** When you see an error message like this, the cell also includes a green triangle in its upper-left corner. Click the cell, and an error button appears to the left of the cell. If you move the mouse pointer over the error button, a ScreenTip displays with a description of what the error means, such as "There is a problem with a number used in the formula."

To see options for dealing with the error, click the error button. A menu of options for addressing the error opens, as shown in Figure 3.10. The choices vary depending on the nature of the error.

The Help on This Error option does the obvious, displaying available help information about the error. Show Calculation Steps opens the Evaluate Formula dialog box, where you can click the Evaluate button to step through the formula and look for a mistake. You also can open the Evaluate Formula dialog box via the Formula Auditing group of the Formulas tab.

3.10 Excel flags a formula error for you and presents choices for resolving the error.

Note The Error Checking choice in the Formula Auditing group of the Formulas tab opens a dialog box that gives some of the same choices that you see when you click a cell's error button.

For some formula errors or in instances where the formula produces an unexpected result that seems off (such as if you get a 0 result when you should get some other value), it might be helpful to look at the precedents (the cells referenced in the formula) and dependents (the other cells with formulas referencing the active cell). To turn on the display of tracing arrows that show precedents or dependents, click Trace Precedents or Trace Dependents in the Formula Auditing group of the Formulas tab. Figure 3.11 shows precedents traced for a formula on a sheet. To remove the tracing arrows from the current sheet, choose Formulas → Formula Auditing → Remove Arrows.

3.11 You can display arrows to trace precedent and dependent cells.

To close the chapter, here's a look at a handful of common formula error messages in Excel:

- **#DIV/0!** The explanation for this one requires one word: impossible. Because it's not possible to divide by 0 (zero) in mathematics, you can't have a formula that divides by 0, so look for that pesky 0 or a divisor cell reference to a cell holding a 0.

- **#N/A!** This means that the formula cannot find the necessary data in a referenced range. This might happen in a formula that uses the HLOOKUP function to find a match for a value in a range of values, and the range with the data to be evaluated is empty.

- **#NUM!** This error message means the formula includes a reference to the wrong type of number, such as when trying to calculate the square root of a negative number using the SQRT function.

- **#REF!** This flags a formula that includes an invalid cell or range reference, such as a reference to a cell on a sheet that doesn't exist in the workbook file.

When Do I Need to Include a Function?

	A	B				G	H
1	Sales and Bonus Calcula						
2							
3	Sales Goal	Bonus Am					
4	$130,000	$3,00					
5							
6	Employee ID	Jan			Total	Average	Bonus?
7	1101	$49,8		,247	$142,205	$47,402	
8	1233	$39,2		,790	$131,775	$43,925	
9	1099	$64,3		,921	$167,868	$55,956	
10	1175	$62,8		,577	$138,490	$46,163	
11	1143	$55,358	$42,587	$32,567	$130,512	$43,504	
12	Total	$271,630	$233,118	$206,102	$710,850	$236,950	
13	Average	$54,326	$46,624	$41,220	$142,170		
14							

Ribbon: File Home Insert Page Layout **Formulas** Data Review View Help

Insert Function ∑ AutoSum ∨ Recently Used ∨ Financial ∨ Logical ∨ Lookup & Reference ∨ n & Trig ∨ e Functions ∨ Name Manager Define Name Use in Formul Create from S Defined Names

Logical dropdown: AND, FALSE, **IF**, IFERR, IFNA, IFS, NOT, OR, SWITCH, TRUE, XOR, *fx* Insert Function...

IF(logical_test,value_if_true,value_if_false)
Checks whether a condition is met, and returns one value if TRUE, and another value if FALSE.
? **Tell me more**

Cell reference: G7

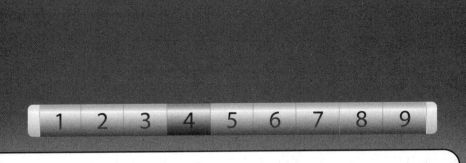

You could spend a lot of time trying to write formulas that use complicated math, but who has extra time on their hands these days? Excel offers hundreds of functions that you can plug in to your formulas to do the math for you. Functions greatly expand what you can do with data, including the ability to look up data or apply a logical test to evaluate data. This chapter introduces you to functions and the various methods for including them in a formula. The chapter concludes by showing you how to use range names with functions and presents some commonly used functions.

Understanding Functions

In Chapter 3, I compared formulas to mini programs. Functions in Excel take that concept a step further. Each function performs a prebuilt calculation or operation, sometimes eliminating the need to enter any math operators at all. The AVERAGE function is a good example. Instead of entering a lengthy formula such as =(C4+C5+C6+C7+C8+C9+C10)/7, you could boil it down to =AVERAGE(C4:C10). The descriptive function names also make the purpose of the sheet easier to follow.

A formula with a function starts with the = (equal) sign like any other formula and includes a pair of parentheses. The items placed between the parentheses with a function are called *arguments*. Arguments can consist of cell and range references, constants, text strings, and range names. A couple of functions don't require arguments at all, while most require at least one argument. Some have required and optional arguments. And still other functions can have more arguments than you'd think. For example, the SUM and AVERAGE functions can have multiple cell or range reference arguments separated by a comma (which is the union operator and is covered in Chapter 3), as in =SUM(B7:B8,D10:D11).

> **! Caution**
>
> Text string arguments must be enclosed with quotation marks. Any comma needed between arguments must be outside the quotation marks. Also note that you do not need to include a space before or after the comma separating two arguments.

For more complex formulas, you can even use a function as one of the arguments for another function, called *nesting* the function. As when a formula includes multiple pairs of parentheses and calculates from the innermost pair out, Excel calculates the nested function(s) first. For example, the formula =IF(SUM(B7:D7)>130000,"Yes","No") first sums the values in the range B7:D7 and then executes the IF function. If the values in B7:D7 total more than 130000 (the logical test), the cell displays Yes (the value if true); for less than or equal to 130000, it displays No (the value if false). IF is one of the logical functions.

Using AutoSum on the Home or Formulas Tab

Excel makes commonly used functions available via the AutoSum button, which appears both in the Editing group on the Home tab and in the Function Library group of the

Formulas tab. The button has the Greek sigma or sum symbol on it on the Home tab and also includes the word *AutoSum* on the Formulas tab. It's also a split button. If you click the left half, Excel starts a formula with the SUM function by default. If you want to choose another function, click the drop-down list arrow on the right side of the button. (Depending on your screen resolution, the button may be split into top and bottom parts, especially on the Formulas tab, so I'll refer to the main part of the button in either case rather than the drop-down list arrow.) The functions available via the AutoSum drop-down list are:

- **SUM.** Sums or adds up the total of the values in the specified range.

- **AVERAGE.** Sums the values in the range and then divides by the number of values to calculate the average.

- **COUNT.** Called Count Numbers on the drop-down list, this function counts the number of value entries in the specified range. You could use it to find the number of samples collected for a scientific study, for example.

- **MAX.** Finds the highest value in the specified range. You might use this function to find the highest month of sales.

- **MIN.** Finds the lowest value in the specified range. This function could be used to find the lowest expense amount in a sheet.

In most cases, you would specify a single range with each of these functions. That said, when you're creating the formula, you also can use the comma between one or more additional cell or range references in between the parentheses. Follow these steps to create a formula with a common function using the AutoSum button:

1. **Click the cell to the right of or below the range that you want to use as the argument.** Excel will automatically suggest the range as the argument for the formula.

2. **Do one of the following:**

   - **Choose Home → Editing → AutoSum (main part of button) or Formulas → Function Library → AutoSum (main part of button).**

   - **Choose Home → Editing → AutoSum (drop-down list arrow) or Formulas → Function Library → AutoSum (drop-down list arrow), and then click the desired function.** Figure 4.1 shows AutoSum on the Formulas tab.

	File	Home	Insert	Page Layout	Formulas	Data	

fx Σ AutoSum ˅   [?] Logical ˅   Lookup & Reference ˅

Insert   Σ Sum   ˅   Math & Trig ˅
Function

Average   e & Time ˅   More Functions ˅

Count Numbers   n Library

B13   Max   *fx*

     Mi̲n

More F̲unctions...

◢			C	D	E
1	Sales				
2					
3	Sales Goal	Bonus Amount			
4	$130,000	$3,000			
5					
6	Employee ID	Jan	Feb	Mar	Total
7	1101	$49,890	$41,068	$51,247	
8	1233	$39,204	$44,781	$47,790	
9	1099	$64,339	$60,608	$42,921	
10	1175	$62,839	$44,074	$31,577	
11	1143	$55,358	$42,587	$32,567	
12	Total	$271,630			
13	Average				
14					

4.1 AutoSum provides a quick way to enter common functions in a formula.

3. **Drag a handle to adjust the selected range as needed or simply drag over the range to select.** For example, in Figure 4.2, I needed to drag a bottom handle up to eliminate the total calculated by another formula in cell B12 from the suggested range. Optionally at this point, you could work within the parentheses to add cell and range references, as shown in the ScreenTip that appears below the cell with the new formula.

4. **Press Enter or Tab to finish entering the formula.** Excel automatically entered the closing parenthesis in the formula for you. Less typing!

Genius

Sometimes Excel flags a formula when there's really no error. For example, if your range argument skips a cell or two immediately above or to the left of the formula entry, the error button may appear to the left of the cell. To tell Excel to stop flagging that error for that cell, click the error button and then choose Ignore Error. Or, you can simply ignore the buttons and green error indicator triangles, as I've done in some figures in this chapter.

| B13 | ▼ | : | × | ✓ | fx | =AVERAGE(B7:B11) | |

◢	A	B	C	D	E
1	Sales and Bonus Calculations				
2					
3	Sales Goal	Bonus Amount			
4	$130,000	$3,000			
5					
6	Employee ID	Jan	Feb	Mar	Total
7	1101	$49,890	$41,068	$51,247	
8	1233	$39,204	$44,781	$47,790	
9	1099	$64,339	$60,608	$42,921	
10	1175	$62,839	$44,074	$31,577	
11	1143	$55,358	$42,587	$32,567	
12	Total	$271,630			
13	Average	=AVERAGE(B7:B11)			
14		AVERAGE(**number1**, [number2], ...)			
15					

Drag a handle to adjust the suggested range.

4.2 You can keep or adjust the range suggested as the argument, or simply drag over the range you want to select.

Typing a Function in a Formula

The earlier description of function arguments may have made you wonder how you're supposed to know which arguments a function requires. Fortunately, as shown in the ScreenTip in Figure 4.2, Excel provides helpful argument prompts when you're using any of the various methods for creating a formula. The prompts show you which arguments to use and in what order they need to be entered for the function to calculate correctly.

If you think you know the exact name of the function that you need and have a rough idea of what arguments it uses, you can simply type the formula in the desired cell or click the cell and then work in the Formula bar. If you're less sure of the formula name and its arguments, you can type the formula anyway. A feature called Formula AutoComplete provides the help you need to finish the formula. Here's how it works:

1. **Click in the cell where you want to enter the formula, or click the cell and click in the Formula bar.**

2. **Type = (equal) plus the first letter or two (or three) of the function name.** As shown in Figure 4.3, a drop-down list with matching functions appears.

3. **Double-click the function to use in the drop-down list.** Optionally, you also can press the down arrow key to select the function in the drop-down list, and then press the Tab key to enter it in the function. Once the function is entered in the formula, the ScreenTip below the formula changes to display the required arguments.

Mar	Total	Average	Bonus?				
$51,247	=su						
$47,790	_fx_ SUBSTITUTE	Replaces existing text with new text in a text string					
$42,921	_fx_ SUBTOTAL						
$31,577	_fx_ SUM						
$32,567	_fx_ SUMIF						
	_fx_ SUMIFS						
	_fx_ SUMPRODUCT						
	_fx_ SUMSQ						
	_fx_ SUMX2MY2						
	_fx_ SUMX2PY2						
	_fx_ SUMXMY2						

4.3 Formula AutoComplete lists matching functions.

Note

As when entering cell and range references, you do not have to type the function name in ALL CAPS when you enter it into the formula. Excel will convert the function name to all caps for you when you finish entering the formula.

4. **Use the mouse or keyboard to enter the specified arguments.** For some functions that require a type of argument that exists either in the program or in the workbook file (such as another function or a range name), AutoComplete displays a list of choices, as shown in the example in Figure 4.4. Double-click the choice to use in the list.

=SUBTOTAL(		
SUBTOTAL(**function_num**, ref1, ...)		
(...) 1 - AVERAGE	˄	
(...) 2 - COUNT		
(...) 3 - COUNTA		
(...) 4 - MAX		
(...) 5 - MIN		
(...) 6 - PRODUCT		
(...) 7 - STDEV.S		
(...) 8 - STDEV.P		
(...) 9 - SUM		
(...) 10 - VAR.S		
(...) 11 - VAR.P		
(...) 101 - AVERAGE	˅	

4.4 The SUBTOTAL function's first argument calls for another function, which you can double-click in the list of allowable choices.

5. **Enter or specify additional arguments as prompted by the ScreenTip, including a comma after each argument except the last one.**

Genius

As you add arguments, the ScreenTip shows the next argument to enter in bold to guide you about what to enter next. Optional arguments have [ ] (square brackets) around them.

6. **Enter the) (closing parenthesis) if needed, and then press Enter or Tab to finish the formula.** In many cases, Excel will let you skip entering the closing parenthesis, but if you get an error message, you may need to go back and add it at the end of the formula.

Note

The #VALUE! error is one of the most common and general errors in Excel and can often happen when a formula performs subtraction or other common math operations but the referenced cells hold text. It also can happen if you enter a date in a format that Excel doesn't recognize—causing Excel to treat it as text rather than as a date entry—and then create a formula that references that cell.

Using the Formulas Tab to Insert a Function

The Function Library group of the Formulas tab on the ribbon provides access to all of Excel's functions. Depending on what online resource you consult, the number of available Excel functions is north of 450 and likely approaching 500. It seems unlikely that even the most avid Excel user has them all committed to memory.

That being the case, the Formulas tab can jump-start you in finding the function you need. You can either browse to find more frequently used functions of a particular type or search for a function if you're not quite sure which function performs the calculation you want.

Choosing from the Function Library

Your local public library helpfully catalogs books by genre for you with signs at the end of the stacks. The signage shows you where to find fiction, nonfiction, reference titles, and books for young adults and children, and some libraries even break it down further from there, with subgroups such as mystery and science fiction. I suspect the Function Library group on the Formulas tab received its name due to its similar organizational structure.

In addition to hosting the AutoSum button you learned about earlier, the Function Library group organizes functions into categories such as Financial, Logical, Text, Date & Time, and more. The Recently Used category includes functions that you've used recently, so it's a go-to category for many users. If you choose More Functions in the group, as shown in Figure 4.5, a menu with additional function categories appears. You can move the mouse pointer over a category in the menu to see the functions in that category.

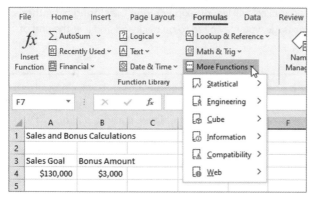

4.5 The Function Library organizes common functions into several categories.

Before you choose a function, first click the cell where you want to insert the formula. Then start looking for a function in the Function Library group of the Formulas tab by choosing the category you think the function is in. If the category has a scrolling list, you may need to scroll down to look for the function you need. To see a ScreenTip describing what a function does, move the mouse pointer over it, as shown in Figure 4.6. Checking out the description gives you a better shot of finding the function you need, rather than just going by memory of what a particular function does.

If you do not find the function you need in the first category you view, no worries. Excel doesn't insert a function until you click it in the category list. So just choose another category and continue until you find the function you want. When you do click a function to choose it, the Function Arguments dialog box shown in Figure 4.7 opens. It lists the arguments for the function and sometimes fills in a suggestion for the first argument for you. If not, you can view the description for the argument lower in the dialog box and enter the required information for the argument. As in similar dialog boxes in Excel, you can type the argument yourself in its text box, or you can use the mouse to specify a cell or range reference. If the cell or range you want is visible, just select it in the sheet. If you can't see the cell or range, click the collapse button at the right end of the argument text box to collapse the dialog box, make the selection, and then click the expand button.

4.6 Each category presents a list of functions.

4.7 The Function Arguments dialog box appears after you insert a function from one of the categories.

Genius

To nest a function in the Function Arguments dialog box, you have to type it as shown for the top argument in Figure 4.7. To verify that nested function arguments or any other arguments are calculating correctly, look at the = expression to the right of the argument text box. For the Logical_test argument shown in the figure, = TRUE to the right is the correct result and an indication that the nested function and its arguments are entered correctly.

When you finish entering one argument, press Tab or click to move to the next argument, checking the description if needed. The name of each required argument appears in bold beside its text box. The other arguments with nonbold names are optional. When you finish entering all the arguments, click OK to finish inserting the formula.

Using Insert Function to find a function

If you'd rather not browse for a function and want to take a more direct route, you can search for a function using the Insert Function dialog box. You don't even have to know the function's name, as the dialog box enables you to search using a description of the calculation or other action you want to perform. Follow these steps to search for a function:

1. **Click the cell where you want to insert the formula with a function.**

2. **Choose Formulas → Function Library → Insert Function or press Shift+F3.** The Insert Function dialog box opens.

Genius

No matter which ribbon tab is currently selected, you can use the Insert Function button on the Formula bar next to the Formula bar text box to open the Insert Function dialog box. The Insert Function button on the Formula bar has the same symbol as the Insert Function button on the Formulas tab.

3. **Type part of the function name or a description in the Search for a Function text box at the top of the dialog box.**

4. **Click the Go button.** As shown in the example in Figure 4.8, the Insert Function dialog box displays possible matches in the Select a Function list.

5. **Double-click the desired function in the Select a Function list or click the function and click OK.** The Function Arguments dialog box opens.

6. **Use the Function Arguments dialog box as described in the previous section to specify arguments and finish entering the formula.**

Insert Function

Search for a function:

Search description ——— Find a value in a list | Go

Or select a category: Recommended

Select a function:

RANK
RANK.AVG
RANK.EQ

Possible matches ———

RANK(number,ref,order)
This function is available for compatibility with Excel 2007 and earlier.
Returns the rank of a number in a list of numbers: its size relative to other
values in the list.

Help on this function | OK | Cancel

4.8 Use the Insert Function dialog box to search for a function.

Genius

Earlier in the chapter, I explained how to tell Excel to ignore an error in a cell. If you've done that but suspect that an ignored error is now creating calculation problems, choose File → Options, choose Formulas at the left side of the Excel Options dialog box, click the Reset Ignored Errors button under Error Checking, and click OK. You also can clear the check box beside Enable Background Error Checking under Error Checking to turn off error indicators altogether.

Using Range Names in Formulas

You can use a range name as an argument for many different types of functions. This enhances the accuracy of your formulas. Not to mention that a formula such as =SUM(NorthOffice) seems more descriptive of the formula's purpose than =SUM(B7:B11). Excel treats range names in formulas as absolute references, so keep that in mind when moving or copying any formula with a range name as an argument. After you create range names in your workbook, you can enter them when creating a formula using any of the main methods discussed in this chapter, as follows:

⦿ **Using AutoSum.** After you choose the function you want using the AutoSum button or list, type the range name between the parentheses and press Enter. Sometimes Excel suggests a range name when you use AutoSum, and if the suggested range name is correct, you can just press Enter to accept it and finish the formula.

● **Typing with Formula AutoComplete.** As you type the formula, when you get to the point where you want to enter the range name as an argument, type the first letter or two. The list of possible matches that Formula AutoComplete displays includes range names, as shown in Figure 4.9. Range names are indicated with a small sheet or grid icon with two blue-shaded cells to the left of the range name. Use the down arrow key to select the range name, and then press Tab to enter it into the formula. Finish the formula from there.

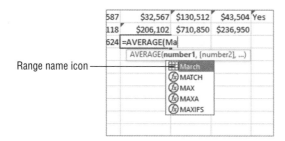

Range name icon

4.9 Formula AutoComplete lists matching range names (among other matches) after you type the first few letters of the name.

● **Using the Function Arguments dialog box.** Type a range name in an argument text box, repeat as needed, and finish creating the formula with the dialog box. For some functions, it might be useful to assign a range name to even a single cell to make it easier to understand the nature of the calculation. For example, for some financial functions, you might create a range name for a cell holding an interest rate or one holding the number of periods in the loan.

Note

The #NAME? error displays in a cell when a formula refers to a range that doesn't exist, or perhaps when the range name has been entered incorrectly. Check and correct any range names used in the formula to clear up this error.

Reviewing Some Essential Functions

I hope that this chapter's introduction to the power of functions has you ready to explore all the possibilities of using single functions to streamline calculations, tapping in to the power of more advanced functions that are right in your career wheelhouse, or combining functions to tackle tedious data operations and free you up for creativity.

You've seen only a few functions so far, and I can't show you all of them in a book like this. The list that follows introduces some functions that can boost your productivity right away. Please enjoy.

- **TODAY.** Entered as =TODAY() with no arguments, this function displays today's date in the cell in the default mm/dd/yyyy format (also called the Short Date format). A date entered this way updates every time you open the workbook file.

- **NOW.** Also entered without arguments as =NOW(), this function displays both the current date and the time in hh:mm format. A date and time entered this way updates every time you open the workbook file as well as while you're making or editing cell entries.

- **DAYS.** This function is used as =DAYS(end_date,start_date) to find the total number of days between the specified dates. For example, let's say you had a project plan with a set start date and end date, and you want to calculate the total number of days for the project. Figure 4.10 shows an example of how you'd do that. You have to enter the dates in cells and use the cell references for the arguments.

B3		⋮	×	✓	fx	=days(B4,B3)	
	A	B	C	D	E		
1	Project Plan						
2							
3	Start Date:	1/3/2022					
4	End Date:	4/8/2022					
5	Days:	=days(B4,B3					
6		DAYS(end_date, start_date)					
7							

4.10 The DAYS function has end_date and start_date arguments.

Note

Chapter 1 explained that when you make a date entry in a format that Excel recognizes, Excel converts the date to a special date serial number. That's why the dates need to be entered in cells rather than typed into the formula. You could perform the same calculation in Figure 4.10 without the DAYS function by typing =B4-B3 in a cell.

- **DATE.** This function returns the date serial number for a date and displays the resulting date in mm/dd/yyyy format, and its syntax is =DATE(year,month,day). Basically, you use the function to combine the parts of the date if the year, month, and day are held in different cells. As for the DAYS function, it's recommended that the arguments be references to cells holding the values you want Excel to evaluate.

● **NETWORKDAYS.** This function is similar to DAYS but returns working days between the start_date and end_date arguments, according to the regular US calendar of a Monday through Friday workweek. It also uses an optional Holidays argument, where you can enter the range reference for a range where you've entered holiday dates, so that a corresponding number of days will be subtracted from the formula result.

● **IF.** You're right, you did see this function briefly earlier in the chapter, in Figure 4.7. This function can display a text result based on a logical test using the comparison operators you learned about in Table 3.1 of Chapter 3. The example workbook you've seen throughout the chapter not only calculates January through March sales totals and averages, but also calculates whether each sales employee sold more than $130,000 (held in cell A4 and referenced in the logical test) to earn a $3,000 bonus. The function's syntax is =IF(logical_test,value_if_true,value_if_false). In Figure 4.7 I entered the logical_test with a nested function, but it also could be entered using a cell reference to a value already calculated in another cell (cell E11 in this example), as shown in Figure 4.11. The value_if_true and value_if_false arguments are optional. If you don't enter them, the formula displays TRUE or FALSE. But if you do want to display other text, enter that text for the optional arguments, using quotation marks. I used "Yes" and "No" in the example.

G11		✕	✓	fx	=IF(E11>A4,"Yes","No")		— IF function

◢	A	B	C	D	E	F	G
1	Sales and Bonus Calculations						
2							
3	Sales Goal	Bonus Amount					
4	$130,000	$3,000					
5							
6	Employee ID	Jan	Feb	Mar	Total	Average	Bonus?
7	1101	$49,890	$41,068	$51,247	$142,205	$47,402	Yes
8	1233	$39,204	$44,781	$47,790	$131,775	$43,925	Yes
9	1099	$64,339	$60,608	$42,921	$167,868	$55,956	No
10	1175	$62,839	$44,074	$31,577	$138,490	$46,163	Yes
11	1143	$55,358	$42,587	$32,567	$130,512	$43,504	Yes
12	Total	$271,630	$233,118	$206,102	$710,850	$236,950	
13	Average	$54,326	$46,624	$41,220			
14							

Cells display Yes or No depending on IF function logical test.

4.11 The IF function performs a logical test and displays a text result.

● **COUNT, COUNTA, and COUNTBLANK.** In a range of cells containing values, COUNT counts the number of cells with values and does not count empty cells or those with other types of entries. This can be useful if you want to know how many answers were given in a survey with answers ranked from 1 through 10, for example. COUNTA counts the number of cells in a range that aren't empty. COUNTBLANK counts empty cells in a range. All three of these functions can come in handy when evaluating large datasets for accuracy and completeness, and are found in the Statistical function category.

- **SUMIF and COUNTIF.** As their names suggest, both of these functions combine their individual action with a test similar to that for an IF function. Both functions have range and criteria arguments, and SUMIF has an optional sum_ range argument.

- **RAND and RANDBETWEEN.** These random number generators can be used to develop sample data or explore potential growth scenarios, among other purposes. Entered as =RAND() with no arguments, this function returns a random number between 0 and 1, so you will often need to multiply the result to arrive at a final random number. The syntax =RANDBETWEEN(bottom,top) requires you to specify the lowest and highest values (or references to cells with values) in order to generate a random number that falls between those two values. (Psst! You don't know that I used RANDBETWEEN to generate the numbers for many of the examples shown in this book's figures.) The results for RAND and RANDBETWEEN update every time you make or edit a cell entry on the sheet, but you can copy the results and use Paste Special (covered in Chapter 2) to paste the results as (static) values rather than updating formulas.

- **ROUND.** This function can come in handy if you have a list of numeric data from another source that has many decimal places. You can use the ROUND function to reduce the number of decimal places displayed while leaving the original values intact. Say the original numbers have five decimal places and are in column A starting with cell A3. In cell B3, you could enter =ROUND(A3,2), with 2 being the number of decimal places to display. Again, you could copy the results and use Paste Special to paste the resulting values (rather than the formulas).

- **VLOOKUP.** This function helps you find a value in a columnar table sorted in ascending order. It finds a value that you specify in the left column (lookup_value argument), searches the table (table_array argument), and then returns a value from the same row as the lookup value in another table column (col_index_num argument). The HLOOKUP function works similarly but looks down the rows (horizontally) rather than across the columns. These functions are part of the Lookup & Reference category.

- **PMT.** If you're shopping for a car or a boat and want to get a sense of how much machine you can afford, the PMT function can help. Its required arguments are rate, nper (number of periods), and pv (present value, or the amount of money you are borrowing). As shown in Figure 4.12, the formula can reference cell entries with values that you can change to see, for example, what your payment would be if you borrow $30,000 versus $40,000. Also notice in the Formula bar that the Rate amount in cell B3 is divided by 12. That's because interest rates are usually stated as an annual rate, but lenders typically then calculate a monthly rate to match the fact that the payments are made monthly (cell B4). Also notice that the formula result appears in parentheses (and it's also red, though you can't see that). This indicates the number is a negative value, which is an accounting convention for cash outflows or payments.

| B7 | ▼ | : | × | ✓ | fx | =PMT(B3/12,B4,B5) |

Annual rate in cell B3 divided by 12 for a monthly rate to match the monthly payments

◢	A	B	C	D	E	F
1	Loan Affordability Check					
2						
3	Rate:	5%				
4	Months:	60				
5	Principal:	$30,000				
6						
7	Payment:	($566.14)				
8						

Result displays as a negative number.

4.12 The PMT function can be used to calculate a loan payment.

- **PROPER.** This function changes the capping for a text string so that the first letter of each word is capitalized. This can be useful for reformatting data from other sources that use all capital letters, which is less readable.

- **CONCAT.** CONCAT works similar to the & concatenation operator mentioned in Chapter 3. It combines multiple text strings from different referenced cells into a single string.

- **LEN.** This function counts the number of characters in a cell, usually for a text string. For example, if you have alphanumeric customer IDs that begin with a letter, Excel treats them as text. Say that all of these customer IDs should be six characters long and that the first ID is in cell A3. You could create a formula with the LEN function in cell B3 to check the length of the first ID [as in =LEN(A3)], copy it down the column, and check for any ID that's not six characters. (The sort and filter features covered in Chapter 7 would help with finding the nonconforming IDs.)

● **LEFT and RIGHT.** These functions also can be useful if you're working with data you've copied or imported from another source. They help you trim a specified number of characters off the entry from the start (RIGHT) or ending (LEFT) of a text string. For example, say a list of product numbers in the range G13:G15 has CA-appended to the beginning, with four numbers after, and you want to get rid of the prefix. The formula to do that would be =RIGHT(G13:G15,4).

How Do I Use Formatting to Enhance My Worksheet?

File	Home	Insert	Page Layout	Formulas	Data	Review	View	Help

Calibri · 11 · | B I U · A^ A^ | General · | Conditional Formatting · | Paste | $ · % 9 | Format as Table · | Cell Styles ·

Clipboard | Font | Alignment | Number | Styles

L17

	A	B	C	D	E	F	G	H	I
1	**Sales and Bonus Calculations**								
2									
3	**Sales Goal**	**Bonus Amount**							
4	$130,000	$3,000							
5									
6	**Employee ID**	**Jan**	**Feb**	**Mar**	**Total**	**Average**	**Bonus?**		
7	1101	$49,890	$41,068	$51,247	$142,205	$47,402	Yes		
8	1233	$39,204	$44,781	$47,790	$131,775	$43,925	Yes		
9	1099	$64,339	$60,608	$42,921	$167,868	$55,956	No		
10	1175	$62,839	$44,074	$31,577	$138,490	$46,163	Yes		
11	1143	$55,358	$42,587	$32,567	$130,512	$43,504	Yes		
12	**Total**	$271,630	$233,118	$206,102	$710,850	$236,950			
13	**Average**	$54,326	$46,624	$41,220					
14									
15									
16									

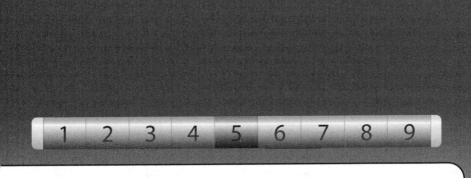

There's no reason to stick with plain, boring worksheets using the default formatting that Excel provides. In contrast, upping your Excel formatting game gives you the opportunity to highlight important cells, make the sheet easier for your readers to understand, and even sprinkle in some organizational branding. This chapter shows you how to apply formatting for worksheet function and flair. The chapter coverage begins with the must-know skill of applying number and date formats. The chapter then reviews key formatting techniques, including working with cell formatting, borders, styles, themes, column width and row height, and conditional formatting.

Changing the Number or Date Format

In a couple of earlier spots in the book, such as the "Number formatting on the fly" section of Chapter 1, I touched on the fact that Excel offers special formats for some types of cell entries, especially numeric and date values. By applying a number format to include a particular symbol and number of decimal places with a cell entry, for example, you can communicate to your readers whether the cell entry is a currency value or a percentage.

When you do not format on the fly when typing in cell entries, you later might need to apply a number format to the cell. The number format indicates more specifically what type of value the cell holds, whether to display a currency or percentage symbol, whether to use the comma thousands separator, and how many decimal places to display.

Excel in most cases applies the default General format to plain cell entries that you make, even for text entries. (One notable exception is that Excel immediately uses the Date or Time number format for recognized dates and times.) You can use the tools in the Number group of the Home tab to change the number format applied to a selected cell or range, in one of three different ways. First, you can click one of the buttons identified in Figure 5.1 to make an immediate formatting change.

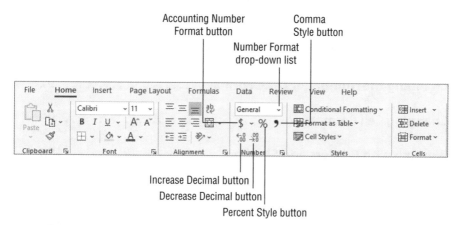

5.1 Use the Number group of the Home tab to change the number format applied to a cell or range.

Genius

The Increase Decimal button displays another decimal place each time you click it, while Decrease Decimal does the opposite. These buttons are the fastest way to adjust the in-cell decimal places displayed with the most common number formats. If you reduce the number of displayed decimal places for a calculated formula result or number, Excel rounds the displayed decimal value up or down as needed.

As shown in Figure 5.1, the Number Format drop-down list displays the name of the currently applied number format, which is the default General format for the selected cell. You can open the drop-down list to apply even more common number formats, as shown in Figure 5.2. One of the nice features of this method is that the list previews each format as it would appear when applied to the current cell. If you look at Figure 5.2, you can see that the Accounting format's preview looks about right, but the Short Date example of 9/6/3851 clearly looks out of whack!

Check the preview for each format.

5.2 The Number Format drop-down list previews various formats for a selected cell.

Finally, you can use the Number tab in the Format Cells dialog box to apply a different number format or to tweak a format, which gives you the most control over how values appear. To open the dialog box, choose More Number Formats from the bottom of the Number Format drop-down list, click the dialog box launcher in the lower-right corner of the Number group of the Home tab, or right-click the selection and choose Format Cells. Choose the approximate type of format you want in the Category list at the left, and then work with the settings that appear to adjust the format as desired. Figure 5.3 shows the available settings for the Number category, which includes choosing whether to include the comma thousands separator and choosing an appearance for negative values in the Negative Numbers list. The Sample area also offers a preview of the current cell's contents. Click OK when you finish choosing a format and its options.

5.3 The Number tab of the Format Cells dialog box offers settings for tweaking a number format.

Using number formats

Now that you know how to apply a number format, it's worthwhile to review when and how to use the various formats. I'll start with the most common formats for numbers, first:

- **Number.** Having a Number number format seems redundant, but the basic flavor of this format displays a number with two decimal places, no thousands separator, and no symbol of any type. (Refer to Figures 5.2 and 5.3.) You might use the Number format for statistical data, but it also can be used in business sheets to reduce the number of currency symbols.

- **Accounting.** The Accounting number format by default adds two decimal places to the number, displays a currency symbol aligned at the far-left side of the cell, and includes the comma thousands separator if applicable. For users in the United States, the $ currency symbol is used. Clicking the main part of the Accounting

Number Format button in the Number group applies the format directly. To display another currency symbol, choose it from the button's drop-down list or use the Format Cells dialog box.

- **Currency.** This format is similar to the Accounting format, but it displays the currency symbol just to the left of the number rather than at the left edge of the cell. This format also gives you additional control over how negative numbers display via the Number tab of the Format Cells dialog box. This format displays zero values as $0.00, while the Accounting format displays zero values as $ - (a currency symbol and a dash). Finally, this format aligns the values all the way to the right side of the cell, while the Accounting format leaves a little space between the right end of the cell entry and the right cell border. Figure 5.4 shows the Currency format used with the Number format to show some financial values.

Number format with
thousands separator   Currency format

	A	B	C	D	E	F	G
1	Sales Comparison						
2							
3	Location	2022	2023	$ Difference	% Difference		
4	N. Charlot	$712,838.00	$708,914.00	-$3,924.00	99.45%		
5	S. Charlot	674,998.00	462,434.00	-212,564.00	68.51%		
6	Winston-S	0.00	487,965.00	487,965.00	N/A		
7	Greensbo	493,046.00	677,701.00	184,655.00	137.45%		
8	Total	$1,882,904.00	$2,339,037.00	-$456,133.00			
9							

Percentage format

5.4 Use number formats to control the display of financial values.

Genius

In some cases, when you apply the Accounting or Currency number format, the added decimal places increase the column width. To avoid the column width change and apply either of these number formats without decimal places, you have to use the Number tab of the Format Cells dialog box. Just select the desired format from the Category list, change the Decimal Places entry to 0, and click OK.

- **Percentage.** When you use the Percent Style button in the Number group of the Home tab, it simply adds the % (percent) sign to the number. If you apply the Percentage number format using the Number Format drop-down list, it adds the

% (percent) sign plus two decimal places, as illustrated in Figure 5.4. Since 1 equals 100% mathematically, make sure you enter the number as a decimal value (.10 for 10 percent) before applying the number format. Or, if the number format changes the number unexpectedly, edit the value after applying the number format.

Caution

Chapter 1 explained that you can type the % (percent) symbol right after a number to format it as a percentage. Excel then treats the number as a decimal (25% is .25) in calculations and applies the Percentage number format. However, when you apply the Percentage number format to a cell holding a whole number with the General number format, Excel treats the entry as a multiple of 100%, so 25 becomes 2500.00%. Clicking the Percent Style button in the Number group does the same, so 25 becomes 2500%.

Using date and time formats

Once Excel correctly recognizes a cell entry as a date or time, you can apply a new format to change the date or time's appearance. If you check back with Figure 5.2, you can see that the Number Format drop-down list offers two number formats using common styles for communicating dates:

- **Short Date.** Displays the date in the 8/1/2023 style.
- **Long Date.** Displays the date in the Tuesday, August 1, 2023 style.

However, you might want to display the date in an even more abbreviated way, such as 1-Aug, or choose a longer format that includes the time, or maybe even use 24-hour military time. Excel offers numerous other number formats in the Date and Time categories of the Number tab of the Format Cells dialog box. Figure 5.5 shows some of the formats in the Date category, and of course, you'd choose Time in the Category list to see the formats for times.

Using special and custom formats

There are some unique situations that come up with certain types of numeric entries. These can happen after you finish an entry, or you might need for Excel to store a number in a different way than normal.

- **Numbers that change to scientific notation after you enter them.** Scientific notation, also called exponential notation, is a shorthand method for displaying long numbers. Excel converts any value you enter with 12 or more digits to scientific notation for display purposes, but the actual Number format remains set to General. For example, if you enter 123456789123456, Excel displays the number as something like 1.23457E+14, rounding the last decimal value. (The number of digits displayed after the decimal point depends on the column width.) The value after the plus indicates how many places to the power of 10 you'd have to adjust the decimal point by (that is, how many places to the right you'd need to move the decimal point) to return to the original number. You can choose the Scientific choice on the Number tab of the Format Cells dialog box to apply the Scientific format to a number with fewer than 12 digits or to control the number of decimal places displayed in the cell.

5.5 You have additional options for formatting dates and times.

● **Numbers that you want to display with punctuation but store without.** Certain types of numbers, such as phone numbers and Social Security numbers, typically appear with punctuation marks such as - (hyphens) and ( ) (parentheses). While these numbers are numeric, they're not used in calculations, but they may be used in other operations such as sorting and filtering (topics covered in Chapter 7). When you're entering numbers like this, it's just easier to skip typing the punctuation. Or, you may be importing lists of these types of numbers from another source like a database, where they also were stored without punctuation. The choices in the

Special category of the Number tab in the Format Cells dialog box enable you to apply a punctuated display format for numbers. It offers these formats: Zip Code, Zip Code + 4, Phone Number, and Social Security Number. Figure 5.6 shows an example of how these formats work.

How the number is entered

How the number displays   Special number formats

5.6 The Special formats change the display for numbers stored without punctuation.

- **Numbers that you want to store as text.** You got me. In Chapter 1 I said how you could enter a value as text by typing a ' (single quote mark), but I didn't really explain why you'd need to do that. One of the prime reasons to do so is if you want to prevent Excel from displaying the number as scientific notation or if you want to prevent Excel from rounding. Excel can only display 15 digits with precision and will round down digits 16+ to 0. That doesn't work if you want to display a 16-digit credit card number or a longer customer account number. If you don't use the ' (single quote) to make the entry, you have to format the cell or range with the Text "number" format *before* you type the entries. (Otherwise, Excel just converts a value displayed as scientific notation to text in scientific notation.) To apply the Text format to a cell or range, go to the Number tab of the Format Cells dialog box, click Text in the Category list, and then click OK. Or, open the Number Format drop-down list in the Number group of the Home tab, scroll down the list if needed, and click Text.

Creating a Custom Number Format

If none of the formats you've scanned so far on the Number tab of the Format Cells dialog box looks the way you want, you can click Custom in the Category list, select a similar format to use as a starter for a custom entry, and then edit the entry in the Type text box. For example, you could choose #,##0.00 near the top of the list and edit it to $#,##0.00" USD" to add the dollar sign and a space plus USD (for US dollars) at the end of the number format. Some of the symbols and punctuation used look a little cryptic, so keep trying until the Sample displays correctly. You also can search Help for "Review guidelines for customizing a number format" and then read the Help article of the same name for a more complete explanation and examples of creating custom number formats.

Changing Cell Formatting

Every new workbook file uses default formatting for cell entries: 11 pt. Calibri font. Yawn. When every cell looks the same, it's not only boring, but it's also a problem, because users of your worksheet can't tell which information in the sheet is most important. Ask yourself, do they want to review each and every individual number, or do they want to jump right to the bottom-line calculation? Formatting can help provide a road map through the sheet's contents.

This section of the chapter introduces you to what's sometimes called *direct* or *manual* formatting in Excel, where you pick and choose the specific combination of formatting settings that you want and apply them one at a time. I'll cover one group of settings here and then cover a few more settings in the next section, "Working with Borders and Shading."

As for the number formats, you can use ribbon choices for applying the setting; click a dialog box launcher to open the Format Cells dialog box to the appropriate tab; or right-click a selection, choose Format Cells, and go to the desired tab.

Genius

Keep in mind that less can be more when it comes to any type of worksheet formatting. Good design sometimes means editing *yourself* and keeping your formatting choices sleek and simple, using formatting selectively, for emphasis. Emphasizing everything means that nothing is really emphasized. Some design experts recommend emphasizing 10 percent or less of the text in any document.

Applying font formatting

The Home tab of the ribbon presents most of the direct formatting choices in the Font and Alignment groups. Figure 5.7 identifies the choices in the Font group that apply to the text, value, or dates held within a selected cell (or range), rather than the cell itself. If you've worked with text formatting in other programs, some of this will be familiar, so I'll just cover the highlights.

The font refers to the overall style of the letters and numbers in a cell. As its name suggests, you use the Font drop-down list to choose the font that you want to apply to a selected cell or range. When you open the Font drop-down list and move the mouse pointer over a font, Excel displays a Live

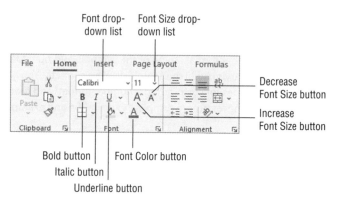

5.7 The Font group holds choices for adjusting the appearance of the text, value, or date in a cell.

Preview of how the font would look if you applied it to the selected cell or range, as shown in the example in Figure 5.8. You could then click the font to apply it to the selection. Newer versions of Excel also offer a feature called *cloud fonts*. These fonts don't initially install with Excel and have a cloud icon beside them in the Font drop-down list. Clicking one of these fonts downloads and installs it on your computer, making it available for use in Excel and other Microsoft 365 applications.

What Do I Need to Know About Font Types?

Generally speaking, there are two different types of fonts: serif (which have small strokes at the end of the letters) and sans serif. (Some fonts with really crazy serifs can be considered a different class of font referred to as a *decorative font*.) Excel's default Calibri font is an example of a sans serif font. Serif fonts are generally considered to be more readable because the serifs guide the eye between characters. They are also thought of as more formal, and some in the design community pooh-pooh them as being too old school. Don't let that prevent you from using serif fonts when appropriate. When you want your worksheet to look more formal or have a packed sheet that you want to ensure is readable, try a serif font or two before just going with a sans serif font. Design experts also advise using only two different fonts overall—one for headings and one for other content. If you must use a third font, use it sparingly.

Indicates a cloud font

Live Preview in selected cell

Mouse pointer over the font to preview

5.8 Check the Live Preview of the font choice in the cell or selection.

The other formatting choices shown in Figure 5.7 are fairly self-explanatory. Use the Font Size drop-down list to change the size of the entry in pt (points, with 72 points per inch). Either you can open the list and click a size or you can change the entry in the Font Size text box and press Enter. The Bold, Italic, and Underline buttons apply (or remove) the specified type of formatting to the selection. The keyboard shortcuts for these three buttons are Ctrl+B, Ctrl+I, and Ctrl+U, respectively. The Underline button also includes a drop-down list that you can use to change between regular single Underline and Double Underline. In accounting documents, it's typical to use single underline formatting for subtotals and double underline formatting for grand totals. Use bold, italics, and underlining sparingly to emphasize content such as headings, as overuse of these types of formatting can make a sheet look cluttered.

Genius

With a 3-D selection (a selection spanning multiple sheets as explained in Chapter 1), any formatting changes you make apply to all the sheets. Say you are creating a workbook to track sales information from three stores. You want each store's sales to be on a separate sheet, but you also want the sheets to have identical layout and formatting. After you add the sheets, you could use 3-D selections when you make entries and apply formatting to save time and get consistent content, appearance, and branding.

You can click the Increase Font Size or Decrease Font Size button to adjust text size. Each click increases or decreases the size to the next size listed on the Font Size drop-down list. Cell contents with a larger font size tend to stand out more. As with other types of formatting, limiting the number of font sizes used on each sheet will avoid a cluttered or overdesigned appearance.

Font Color is another split button. The left side of the button displays a font color, and clicking that part of the button applies the color to the contents of the selected cell or range immediately. To choose another color, click the drop-down list arrow on the right side of the button. A gallery or palette of colors appears, as shown in Figure 5.9. As for the Font drop-down list, moving the mouse pointer over a color in the gallery displays a Live Preview of the color in the contents of the selected cell or range. Click a color to apply it.

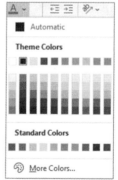

5.9 You can choose another font color for the selected cell or range.

Excel does offer strikethrough, superscript, and subscript formatting via the Font tab of the Format Cells dialog box. To open the dialog box, click the dialog box launcher in the lower-right corner of the Font group on the Home tab, or right-click the selection, click Format Cells, and then click the Font tab. In the Effects area at lower left, use the Strikethrough, Superscript, and Subscript check boxes as needed, and then click OK.

Note

Chapter 9 covers how to add headers and footers that will appear on every page when you print a worksheet. The preset header and footer options in Excel don't include any special formatting. You can format the header and footer contents to a limited degree, with the available choices in the Font group of the Home tab.

Applying alignment formatting

The Alignment group of the Home tab shown in Figure 5.10 offers various tools for changing the vertical and horizontal alignment and indention of cell contents, wrapping and rotating cell contents, and even merging and unmerging cells. Here's a look at what these buttons do to the selected cell or range:

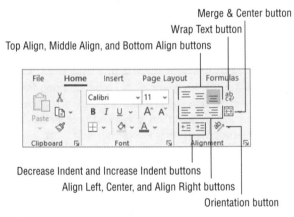

5.10 You can change the alignment, indention, wrapping, and rotation of the contents of a selected cell or range.

- **Top Align, Middle Align, and Bottom Align.** These buttons come into play when the row height has been changed, so you want to choose how the contents should align relative to the top and bottom boundaries of the cell. For example, Middle Align can be a nice choice if you want white space both above and below the cell contents, and if you want to offset the cell contents from the cells above or below.

103

- **Align Left, Center, and Align Right.** These buttons have the most impact when the column is wider than the cell contents and control how the contents align relative to the left and right cell boundaries.

- **Decrease Indent and Increase Indent.** When you want just a little space between the cell boundary and the contents, choose one of these buttons.

- **Wrap Text.** This causes the text to wrap to two or more lines within the cell, based on the column width. To create manual line breaks as you enter text, press Alt+Enter.

- **Merge & Center.** Select a range of cells to merge and then click this button to both merge the cells and center the contents of the leftmost or upper-left cell within the merged area. Merging and centering a title above the range of detailed data gives the sheet a polished look. Clicking the drop-down list arrow for this button displays a menu of additional commands, including Unmerge Cells for returning to a normal range of separate cells.

- **Orientation.** Clicking this button also opens a menu of preset choices for rotating text. If you choose Format Cell Alignment at the bottom of the menu, the Format Cells dialog box opens with the Alignment tab displayed. In addition to using this tab to apply any of the alignment formatting already discussed, you can use the controls in the Orientation area at the upper right to set a custom rotation for a selection.

Genius

You can use the Format Painter to copy number and cell formatting from one selection to another. Select the cells with the formatting to copy, choose Home ➔ Clipboard ➔ Format Painter, and then drag over the other cells to format. You also can double-click the Format Painter button to lock it on, click or drag to copy the formatting to multiple other locations, and then press Esc or click the button again to turn off Format Painter.

Figure 5.11 shows a number of formatting selections from the Font and Alignment groups of the Home tab applied in an example worksheet, for a sense of the possibilities. Some of the changes are obvious, such as the fact that I applied a different font to the title and labels in the sheet and increased the font size for the title. I changed the font color for all the total values to green and all the average values to blue. I wrapped some titles, used a preset to rotate others, and applied both vertical and horizontal centering to offset some labels from the values below them. Finally, the left-aligned text entries for the Bonus? column looked too crowded next to the right-aligned values in the Average column, so I used the Increase Indent button to add just enough space to make the Bonus? column more clean and readable.

Angle Counterclockwise preset applied

Wrapped labels

A1:G1 merged and centered

	A	B	C	D	E	F	G
1	**Sales and Bonus Calculations**						
2							
3	**Sales Goal**	**Bonus Amount**					
4	$130,000	$3,000					
5							
6	**Employee ID**	*Jan*	*Feb*	*Mar*	**Total**	**Average**	**Bonus?**
7	1101	$49,890	$41,068	$51,247	$142,205	$47,402	Yes
8	1233	$39,204	$44,781	$47,790	$131,775	$43,925	Yes
9	1099	$64,339	$60,608	$42,921	$167,868	$55,956	No
10	1175	$62,839	$44,074	$31,577	$138,490	$46,163	Yes
11	1143	$55,358	$42,587	$32,567	$130,512	$43,504	Yes
12	**Total**	$271,630	$233,118	$206,102	$710,850	$236,950	
13	**Average**	$54,326	$46,624	$41,220			
14							

Indented

Middle Align and Center applied

5.11 I've applied various formatting settings to enhance this example worksheet.

Working with Borders and Shading

The additional direct formatting choices covered in this section apply to the cell itself, rather than the text, value, or date within the cell. You can think of this as formatting the container or background for the sheet information. The last two buttons in the Font group of the Home tab are the Fill Color button (which is next to the Font Color button and has a paint bucket icon on it) and the Borders button (which initially displays a grid with a bottom underline on it). Using these buttons, you can create dimension and contrast between cells on the sheet or highlight information in a particular way.

The Fill Color button works just like the Font Color button, except that it applies a fill or background color (also called *cell shading*) to the selected cell or range. You can click the

Genius

If you click the Select All button where the row numbers and column letters meet, you can apply a background fill color to all the cells in the sheet. A fill created in this way does print, but only within the selected print area and margins. Chapter 9 covers printing. You also can select a page background image using the Page Layout → Page Setup → Background choice, but this type of background only appears on-screen and does not print.

left or main part of the button to apply the currently displayed color. To apply another color, click the drop-down list arrow on the right side of the button, move the mouse pointer over various colors to see Live Preview of the color on the selection, and then click the color you ultimately want.

By default, clicking the Borders button applies a bottom border to the selected range (but not the individual cells in the range). That said, you can apply any of a number of different border presets by clicking the drop-down list arrow for the Borders button and then choosing a preset style to use. Choices include Outside Borders (a box around the outside of the selected range), Top and Bottom Border, Top and Thick Bottom Border, and of course, No Border, which removes any previously applied border. Use the Line Color and Line Style submenu choices to make the border less plain. Choosing More Borders from the bottom of the menu opens the Format Cells dialog box with the Border tab displayed, as shown in Figure 5.12.

Use the Border tab to choose multiple settings to apply at once in the selected range. In the Line box, choose from the Style list, and then use the Color drop-down list to choose

Note

As covered in the "Changing views" section in Chapter 1, you might want to toggle gridline display off so that the gridlines don't visually compete with the fills and borders you've applied on the sheet. You also can turn off the display of the Formula bar and column and row headers (or headings) for the cleanest look for a finalized file. These settings are in the Show group of the View tab.

a line color. Then, you can apply the line in one of three ways. You can click one of the three buttons under Presets. You can click directly on the preview to apply a border to the desired location. Or, you can click one of the Border buttons surrounding the preview to choose the border position. Click OK to apply your final choices.

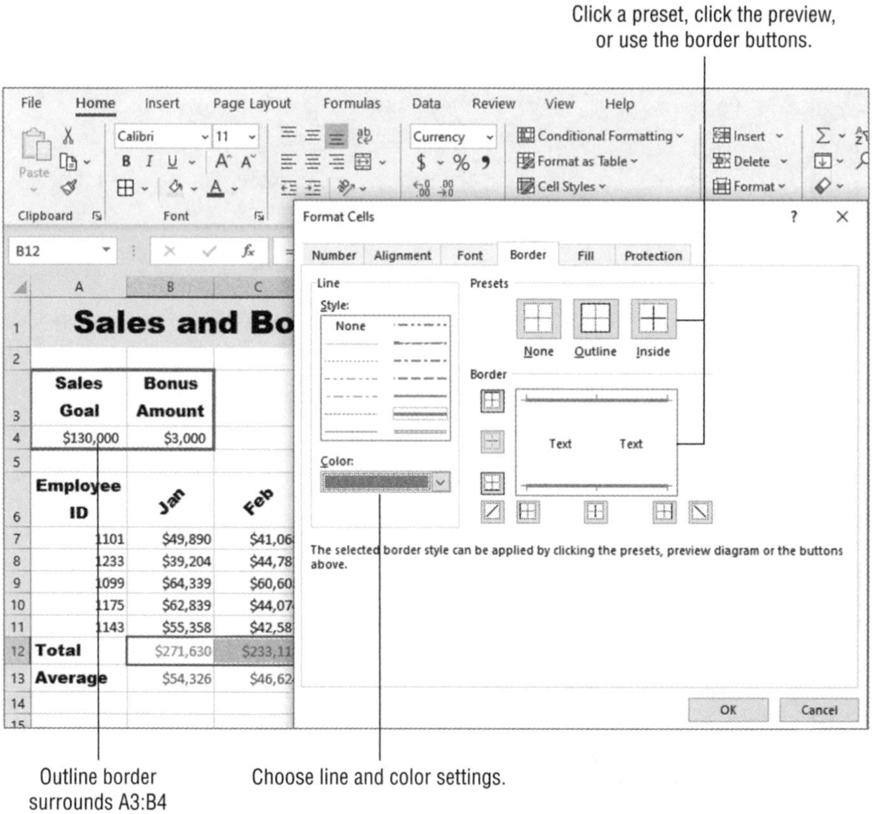

Click a preset, click the preview,
or use the border buttons.

Outline border
surrounds A3:B4

Choose line and color settings.

5.12 You can apply multiple border settings at once using the Border tab.

Using Styles

If you're not into spending time overthinking what combination of cell formatting and borders to apply to various cells and ranges in a worksheet, you can instead opt to use the Home → Styles → Cell Styles gallery shown in Figure 5.13. Move the mouse pointer over a style to see a Live Preview in the selected cell or range, and then click the style you want to use.

In the example in the figure, I've applied the Title style to the contents of cell A1, the Input Style to B3:B5, and 40% shaded accent colors to A3:A5 and A7. I'm in the process of applying the Output style to cell B7.

Using cell styles provides the same advantages of using styles in a word processing document. They are already designed for you, so you don't have to try endless combinations

Loan Affordability Check

	A	B	C	D	E
1	Loan Affordability Check				
2					
3	Rate:	5%			
4	Months:	60			
5	Principal:	$30,000			
6					
7	Payment:	($566.14)			

B7 =PMT(B3/12,B4,...

Cell Styles gallery:

Good, Bad and Neutral

Normal | Bad | Good | Neutral

Data and Model

Calculation | Check Cell | Explanatory ... | Input | Linked Cell | Note

Output | Warning Text

Titles and Headings

Heading 1 | Heading 2 | Heading 3 | Heading 4 | Title | Total

Themed Cell Styles

20% - Accent1	20% - Accent2	20% - Accent3	20% - Accent4	20% - Accent5	20% - Accent6
40% - Accent1	40% - Accent2	40% - Accent3	40% - Accent4	40% - Accent5	40% - Accent6
60% - Accent1	60% - Accent2	60% - Accent3	60% - Accent4	60% - Accent5	60% - Accent6
Accent1	Accent2	Accent3	Accent4	Accent5	Accent6

Number Format

Comma | Comma [0] | Currency | Currency [0] | Percent

New Cell Style...
Merge Styles...

Output style being applied

5.13 Find predefined formatting in the Cell Styles gallery.

Caution Any direct formatting that you apply from the Font or Alignment groups on the Home tab overrides the applicable style formatting, such as the style's cell fill color or applying italics when the style calls for regular text. Reapply the style to remove the direct formatting.

of font, size, color, fill, and borders. If you stick with using the cell styles for the majority of your worksheets—especially the ones that identify specific actions such as Input, Calculation, Note, or Warning Text—you'll produce sheets that are more attractive, usable, and consistent. Even better, if you apply a different theme to the workbook file, any cells formatted using the choices under Themed Cell Styles update automatically. (I cover themes shortly.) If you give cell styles a try, I predict you'll stick with them.

Clearing Formatting

Sometimes it's harder to back up than to go forward. You may have changed various formatting settings applied to a selection here and there, and now you can't remember exactly what you did. In this situation, the ability to clear formatting from a cell or range saves the day. It's an easy two-step process:

1. **Select the cell or range with the formatting to clear.**

2. **Choose Home → Editing → Clear → Clear Formats.** This leaves the cell contents in place while removing the formatting, including the number format.

The Clear menu includes other choices. Another useful one in the bunch is Clear All, which removes both the cell contents and the formatting. Using Clear All can help if you think previously applied formatting such as a number format might introduce an error if you later make another entry in the cell.

Understanding Themes

A theme is a collection of colors, fonts, and effects settings that you can apply to a workbook file. Each new blank workbook you create in Excel uses a theme called Office Theme by default. When you change from one theme to another, Excel applies the new theme's colors, fonts, and effects throughout the workbook file. Using the same theme for all your business workbooks also can help build a recognizable brand in the minds of your customers and colleagues, so it's worth the time to learn more about this perhaps underused formatting feature in Excel.

Reviewing elements of a theme

Each theme offers a specific collection selected to work well together and lend a consistent, attractive design. The combination of design choices in each theme also suggests, well, a theme or mood for the workbook. For example, if you work in the finance or banking field, you might use the Dividend theme. Those in science or aviation might try the Celestial or Vapor Trail theme. There are more than 30 themes that install with Excel.

Each theme consists of the following three design elements:

- **Theme colors.** Each theme has a palette of 12 colors, some of which are used in specific instances or used along with cell styles. The first four are dark and light variations for text and backgrounds. Then there are six accent colors. The final two are a color for hyperlink cell entries and followed hyperlinks.

- **Theme fonts.** The theme fonts specify the heading font and body font. The heading font is used with the heading cell styles, while the body font is used for cell entries that don't have a heading style applied.

- **Theme effects.** The theme effects provide formatting for objects such as shapes and SmartArt, which are covered in Chapter 6. The effects include fills, shadows, border styles, and shading that change the look of graphics.

Changing themes

The Page Layout tab of the ribbon includes many of the settings that affect overall sheet or workbook design, including the settings for themes in the Themes group. If you move the mouse pointer over the Themes button in the group, a ScreenTip showing the name

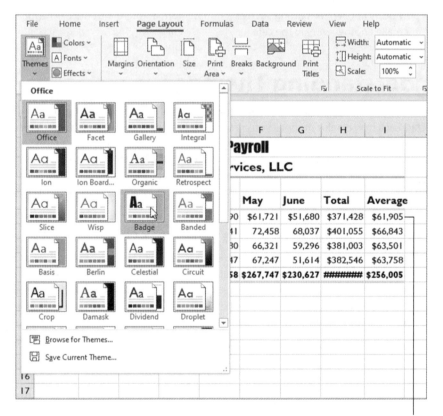

5.14 Change the workbook theme in the Themes gallery.

Note

Some downloadable templates include custom themes that you may want to review to cue your own choices for colors and fonts.

of the currently applied theme appears. Follow these steps to change the theme used by the workbook file:

1. **Choose Page Layout → Themes → Themes to open a gallery of the available themes.**

2. **Move the mouse pointer over a theme to display a Live Preview.** See Figure 5.14.

3. **Click the theme you want to apply.**

If you look at a few spots in Figure 5.14, you'll see that the # (pound) signs appear in cell H9, and the heading label in cell I4 no longer fits within the cell. Excel usually adjusts little things like that for you, but you should still check all the sheets in the file to see if you need to make any formatting adjustments after changing the theme.

Changing theme colors, fonts, and effects

While using the same theme for all of your workbook files helps with consistency, you don't need to take that to the point of boring sameness. For example, you might want

Genius

Use the Page Layout → Themes → Colors → Customize Colors and Page Layout → Themes → Fonts → Customize Fonts commands to create custom combinations of theme colors and theme fonts. And apply another theme effects if desired. Then choose Page Layout → Themes → Themes → Save Current Theme to save those settings as a custom theme. Creating a custom theme can enhance branding beyond just using the same theme.

to use different colors in a file performing calculations for a new brand or try on different fonts for workbooks from the marketing department. You can change the current theme colors, theme fonts, or theme effects.

If you move the mouse pointer over the Colors, Fonts, or Effects buttons in the Themes group of the Page Layout tab, a ScreenTip showing you the name of the currently applied theme element appears. By default, this matches the currently applied theme, so the default theme fonts for the Office theme are the Office theme fonts.

To change any of these theme items, click its button in the Page Layout → Themes group. Each of the galleries that appears offers the Live Preview feature, as shown in Figure 5.15.

When you like the Live Preview of a particular choice, click it. If you compare the fonts shown in Figure 5.15 to those used in Figure 5.14, you can get a sense of how dramatically changing a theme element can update the look of the contents in a workbook file.

Theme fonts Live Preview

5.15 You can choose different theme fonts, as well as different theme colors and effects.

Note

The series of pound signs filling a cell is sometimes called a *hash tag error*, because the # (pound) sign is also known as a hash sign and used in hash tags.

Working with Column Width and Row Height

I mentioned earlier that when you apply some number formats or other formatting, Excel automatically adjusts the column width and sometimes the row height. When you're entering data, however, this isn't the case. If you make a text entry that's too wide for the cell and there's an entry in the cell to the right, the text entry can't fully display and is cut off at the right. Or you may see ##### (a series of pound signs) within a cell holding a value or formula, which means the number is too wide to display in the column. (The number is still there; you just can't see it at the moment.) You also might just want to adjust row height or column width to suit your own taste and add some spacing between

Caution | Given that it's typical to enter the title for a worksheet in cell A1 and worksheet titles can get pretty long, you probably don't want to double-click the column A heading border to widen the column because you'd end up with a massively wide column. Dragging the border or using another method gives you more precision.

information in various rows or columns of the sheet, as illustrated earlier in Figure 5.11.

There are at least four ways to change the column width or row height, and the best method to use depends on whether you want to resize one row or column at a time or select multiple rows or columns and resize them to the same size for consistency. Here are three main methods, along with my thoughts on when it's best to use each:

- **Double-clicking the column header or row header divider.** If you move the mouse pointer over the divider line to the right of the column letter or below the row number, the mouse pointer changes to a black double-headed arrow with a vertical or horizontal line through it (see Figure 5.16). When you see that pointer, you can double-click the divider line, and Excel snaps the column width or row height to the optimal size for the cell contents. This is my preferred technique in most cases given its no-brainer appeal. Excel even calls this feature AutoFit, appropriately.

- **Drag the column header or row header divider.** Do the same maneuver with the mouse to get the special pointer, and then drag the column or row divider until the column or row reaches the size you want. As you drag, a ScreenTip shows you the current Width or Height, displaying both character and pixel values for Width and pt (point) and pixel values for Height. This method works fine if you just need for

Resizing pointer

Rows selected for resizing

5.16 Changing column width or row height can help cell entries display properly and add spacing to the layout of information in a sheet.

cell contents to display correctly but aren't trying for a precise column width or row height, which is more difficult to achieve when dragging.

● **Using the Column Width or Row Height dialog box.** If you want to set multiple columns or rows to a uniform width or height, this is the way to go. It also works for a single column or row. Start by selecting the column(s) or row(s) to adjust. Then, either right-click the header and choose Column Width or Row Height, or choose Home → Cells → Format → Column Width or Home → Cells → Format → Row Height. Enter or change the Column Width or Row Height text box value as applicable (character values for column widths and pt values for row height), and then click OK. Figure 5.16 shows the Row Height dialog box as an example.

Using Conditional Formatting to Highlight Information

When I'm geeking out over my data, I like to try conditional formatting to see what significant data points I can uncover. Conditional formatting applies different formatting to cells based on rules and comparisons between the different values. With conditional formatting, you can:

Color scale changes cell fill colors based on cell values.

5.17 The Conditional Formatting menu offers dozens of choices grouped into submenus.

- **Highlight cells in a selected range based on comparisons, text, or dates.**

- **Identify values that are top, bottom, or above or below average in a selected range.**

- **Show how values compare with data bars, color scales, or icon sets in a selected range.**

There are dozens of conditional formatting choices, so this is another feature to explore when you have a little free time on your hands. There are two ways to apply conditional formatting, both of which (usually) provide a Live Preview of the formatting that will be applied to the selected range:

Icon set displayed with values

	A	B	C	D	E	F	G	H	I	J
1				**First Half Payroll**						
2				**2Day Tech Services, LLC**						
3										
4	**Location**	**January**	**February**	**March**	**April**	**May**	**June**	**Total**	**Average**	
5	N. Charlotte	$61,994	$61,689	$60,654	$73,690	$61,721	$51,680	⬇ $371,428	⬇ $61,905	
6	S. Charlotte	67,080	57,602	63,437	72,441	72,458	68,037	⬆ $401,055	⬆ $66,843	
7	Winston-Salem	63,364	69,701	50,541	71,780	66,321	59,296	⬇ $381,003	⬇ $63,501	
8	Greensboro	56,366	68,436	71,936	66,947	67,247	51,614	➡ $382,546	➡ $63,758	
9	**Total**	**$248,804**	**$257,428**	**$246,568**	**$284,858**	**$267,747**	**$230,627**	536,032	**$256,005**	
10										
11					Formatting	Charts	Totals	Tables	Sparklines	
12										
13										
14					Data Bars	Color...	Icon Set	Greater...	Top 10%	Clear...
15										
16										
17					Conditional Formatting uses rules to highlight interesting data.					
18										
19										

Quick Analysis button

5.18 Quick Analysis narrows down the conditional formatting choices.

Note

You also can create your own custom rules for conditional formatting, such as if you want to use custom colors for color scales. Just choose More Rules or New Rule anywhere you see it on the Conditional Formatting menu or a submenu to get started.

● **Choose Home → Styles → Conditional Formatting, and then work from there.**
As shown in Figure 5.17, each type of conditional formatting displays its own submenu, and you can explore the Live Preview of the choices before clicking the one to apply.

● **Select and move the mouse pointer over the range, click the Quick Analysis button that appears at the lower-right corner (or press Ctrl+Q), and work from there.** Quick Analysis narrows the conditional formatting offerings down to a few recommended choices, so you can quickly choose one that works for your data (see Figure 5.18).

How Do I Use Graphics in Excel?

	Device	Watts	Hours Per Day	Watt-Hours Per Day				
	Business Energy Consumption							
	Lighting	100	9	900				
	Laptop	50	4	200				
	Computer monitor and tower	270	3	810				
	Inkjet printer	30	2	60				
	Phone charger	4	4	16				

Infographics combine text, graphics, and charts to simplify or summarize an idea or concept. What does that have to do with Excel, you ask? Many infographics present data and statistics—you know, the type of information you may be developing in your worksheets. You can include graphics on a sheet to add your organization's logo, highlight important values or takeaways, show a product image, or even illustrate a process. This chapter shows you how to insert and edit various types of graphics to make the info in your sheets more memorable.

Inserting Simple Graphics

Excel offers a variety of types of graphics that you can add to a worksheet. Unsurprisingly, you can find the choices for inserting various types of graphics in the Illustrations group of the Insert tab, shown in Figure 6.1. The rest of this section shows you how to add the various types of graphics and provides examples of when you might use each type. You'll learn a little later in the chapter how to move, size, and otherwise format graphics after you've inserted them.

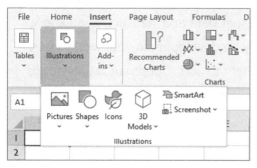

6.1 Use the Illustrations group of the Insert tab to add graphics to a sheet.

Note

Figure 6.1 is a good example of an instance where screen resolution makes a big difference in the ribbon layout. If you're working at a higher resolution, the Illustrations group will not be collapsed down to a button, as shown in Figure 6.1. At a higher resolution, the Pictures, Shapes, Icons, and SmartArt buttons appear directly on the ribbon in the Illustrations group.

Shapes

Choosing the Shapes button in the Illustrations group of the Insert tab opens the drop-down gallery shown in Figure 6.2. The gallery groups the shapes by type, and you can scroll down if needed to view additional shapes. You can pause the mouse pointer over a shape to see a ScreenTip with the shape's name, but in most cases, the Shapes button is pretty self-explanatory.

Arrow: Left shape points to highest percentage

File	Home	Insert	Page Layout	Formulas	Data	Review	View	Help

Tables Illustrations Add-ins ˅ Recommended Charts Maps PivotChart 3D Map ˅ Sparklines Filters

Charts Tours

L22

Pictures Shapes Icons 3D Models ˅ SmartArt Screenshot ˅

			D	E	F	G
1	Sa					
2						
3	Location		ference	% Difference		
4	N. Charlotte		-$3,924.00	99.45%		
5	S. Charlotte		-212,564.00	68.51%		
6	Winston-Sale		487,965.00	N/A		
7	Greensboro		184,655.00	137.45%		
8	Total		$456,133.00			
9						
10						
11						
12						
13						
14						
15						
16						
17						
18						
19						
20						
21						
22						
23						
24						

Recently Used Shapes

Lines

Rectangles

Basic Shapes

Block Arrows

Equation Shapes

Flowchart

6.2 Shapes are grouped by type.

To add a shape, in most cases, you click the shape you want in the Shapes gallery and then drag on the worksheet to create a shape that's the size you need. That said, a few tips or exceptions come to mind:

- **Inserting a shape at the default size.** To insert a shape at the default size, which is usually 1" x 1", just click once on the sheet after choosing the shape from the gallery. This works well when you want to insert multiple shapes that are exactly the same size.

- **Inserting a perfect circle or square.** If you choose the Oval or Rectangle shapes, you can press and hold Shift while dragging to create a perfect circle or square.

- **Inserting a curve.** The Curve choice in the Lines section of the Shapes gallery creates a special type of curve called a Bézier curve, which bends around a series of points. After you choose this tool, click to place the first point, click to place additional points, and then double-click the final point.

- **Inserting freeform shapes.** The Lines section also includes Freeform: Shape and Freeform: Scribble choices. After you choose one of these, just drag as you please with the mouse. To finish a filled freeform shape, just move the mouse pointer back over the starting point for the outline you've created, and when you see the fill appear, release the mouse button. For the scribble, just release the mouse button at the end of the scribble.

You can add shapes for purely decorative purposes if you want, but it's even more powerful to use them to highlight important information or add new information that can't be conveyed by a simple label. For example, the arrow in Figure 6.2 points to the highest calculated % Difference. You could similarly use a rectangle, oval, or rounded rectangle shape around key values in a sheet. The Equation Shapes are mathematical operators that could be used to illustrate a calculation. There are Flowchart shapes that could be used along with some of the line and connector shapes in the Lines section of the Shapes gallery to create a process flowchart diagram like the ones traditionally used in the engineering and programming fields, among others.

The gallery also has sections with Stars and Banners and Callouts. A *callout* is a bubble or box with short descriptive text and a line or pointer to what the callout describes. (You've seen a lot of callouts in the figures in this book.) How can an empty shape include descriptive text? A later section in this chapter, "Adding text to shapes," explains how, so you can add text to your sheet's star, banner, or callout shapes.

Pictures

In the past, Excel and the other Microsoft 365 applications limited you to inserting picture or graphic files from your computer. That was adequate if the goal was limited to inserting a company logo or product image. Now Microsoft has incorporated more ways to find and insert graphic files, although you can still insert a file from your computer.

The newest addition is the availability of stock images—images that you can use in your worksheets and other documents without the need to hire a photographer or graphic designer. Stock image providers usually charge a fee or royalty, but Microsoft offers its collection of stock images for royalty-free use to its Microsoft 365 subscribers. The stock images fall into five categories: Images, Icons (which I'll cover separately a little later), Cutout People, Stickers and Illustrations. Here's how to insert a stock image, which requires that your computer be connected to the Internet:

1. **Choose Insert → Illustrations → Pictures → Stock Images.** A window that you can use to search for stock images appears, as shown in Figure 6.3. The Images category is selected by default. The pictures you see and the search terms below the Search box vary each time you open the window, so your screen will differ accordingly from Figure 6.3.

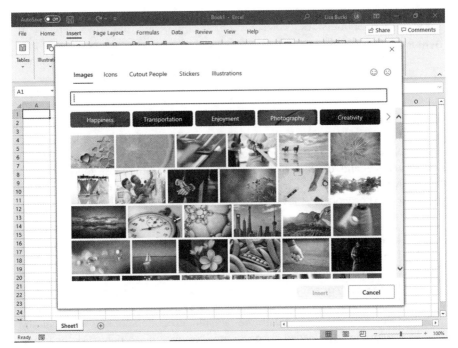

6.3 Thousands of royalty-free stock images are available to insert on your worksheets.

2. **If needed, click one of the other categories at the top of the window.**

3. **Browse or search for images, as follows:**

    - Scroll the search terms below the Search box to the right or left using the arrows, and then click a term. Pause until matching images appear.

    - Click in the Search box, type a search term or phrase, and either press Enter or pause until matching images appear.

4. **Scroll down through the pictures if needed, and then click the thumbnail for the picture to insert so that a green check circle appears in its upper-right corner.** Optionally, you can select multiple images. The Insert button shows the number of selected images in parentheses, as in (2).

5. **Click the Insert button.** The selected image downloads and appears on the worksheet, usually near the location of the active cell.

Genius

Other sources of stock imagery include iStock (`www.istockphoto.com`) and Shutterstock (`www.shutterstock.com`). These two services in particular offer some images that are royalty-free after you pay a fee or purchase a subscription. There are many other sources for free graphics; just make sure you choose a reputable source and scan downloaded files for viruses.

The Insert ➔ Illustrations ➔ Pictures ➔ Online Pictures choice uses a search engine to find other pictures on the Internet for you. In the Online Pictures window that appears, type a search word or phrase in the Search box and press Enter. Figure 6.4 shows the Online Pictures window and identifies a few key features. Perhaps the most important one is the Creative Commons Only check box. I recommend you leave this checked so that you know you won't be violating the image creator's copyright.

Note

Creative Commons (CC) is an organization and framework for licensing copyright protected works for free. The six main license levels, all of which require attribution be given to the image's creator, are described at `https://creativecommons.org/about/cclicenses`. Some creators choose to release content under less restrictive public domain licenses. Sometimes a caption with the required attribution appears automatically with the downloaded image. In other cases, you can right-click the image and click View Source to identify the license and any required attribution.

If you move the mouse over any image thumbnail, the More Information and Actions button (with three dots on it) appears in the lower-right corner of the thumbnail. Click it to see more information about the image, such as the image size or sometimes a link to the source image online. Clicking the Filter button opens a scrolling list of categories by which you can filter the matches, including Size, Type, Layout, and Color. Just make the choices you need in each category, such as choosing Small under Size, which requires clicking the Filter button again for each filter to apply. Or, choose Clear All Filters at the bottom of the list to remove previously applied filters.

Filter button

Creative Commons Only check box

Selected image

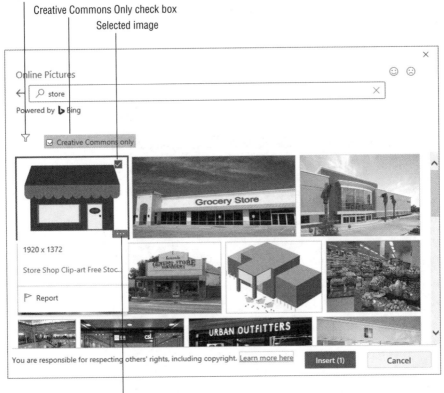

More Information and Actions button

6.4 Online Pictures uses a search engine to search the Internet for matching images.

To select an image to download, click its thumbnail so that a green check box appears in its upper-right corner. Then click Insert to download the image, which again appears near the active cell. Figure 6.5 shows a sheet with both a stock image and an online picture. I've increased the transparency of the stock image so that I could position it to look like it's behind the sheet contents. I've made the online picture smaller so that I could position it above the data. I just wanted to give you a taste of the formatting possibilities I show you later in the chapter.

Finally, inserting a graphic file stored on your computer, an external network drive, or USB flash drive works much like opening a workbook file. Choose Insert → Illustrations → Pictures → This Device, navigate to the location holding the image file in the Insert Picture dialog box that appears, select the picture, and click Insert. You can insert pictures from many common graphics file formats, including JPEG, PNG, TIFF, and more. Only files using one of the allowable formats appear in the Insert Picture dialog box. You would use this technique to insert your company logo or a digital photo you've taken of a product.

Online picture

▲	A	B	C	D	E
1	Sales Comparison				
2					
3	Location	2022	2023	$ Difference	% Difference
4	N. Charlotte	$712,838.00	$708,914.00	-$3,924.00	99.45%
5	S. Charlotte	674,998.00	462,434.00	-212,564.00	68.51%
6	Winston-Salem	0.00	487,965.00	487,965.00	N/A
7	Greensboro	493,046.00	677,701.00	184,655.00	137.45%
8	Total	$1,882,904.00	$2,339,037.00	$456,133.00	
9					
10					
11					
12					
13					
14					
15					
16					
17					
18					
19					

Stock image

6.5 This sheet has a stock image and an online picture.

Icons

If you really want to add an infographic feel to a worksheet, try adding icons. Icons are part of the royalty-free stock imagery now offered to Microsoft 365 subscribers. Choose Insert ➔ Illustrations ➔ Icons to open the stock image window with the Icons category selected at the top, as shown in Figure 6.6. As you saw earlier for stock images, you can either enter a search term or scroll through the search terms below the box and click one. (The icons and search terms you see will vary.) Scroll down if needed, and then click the thumbnail for the icon to insert so that a green check circle appears in its upper-right corner. Then click Insert.

The icons you insert can be edited like other graphics, and not just the icon size. You can change other settings such as fill and line colors, too. See the later section called "Changing styles" to learn more.

6.6 You can search for an icon to add in this window.

Note

The Illustrations group also includes choices for inserting 3-D models and a screenshot. A 3-D model can be used for more technical types of worksheets, such as those tracking product dimensions. You can create a screenshot or screen clipping from another open program, which automatically places it on the current sheet. You might use a screenshot to document sources for worksheet values, for example.

Selecting and Formatting Graphics

In most cases, you can simply click an inserted graphic of any type to select it. You can Shift+click or Ctrl+click when you need to select multiple graphics, such as when you need to align them or want to apply similar formatting.

When a graphic is selected, a tab with formatting settings—sometimes called a *contextual tab* or a *context-sensitive tab*—appears on the ribbon, usually to the far right. The name of this contextual tab varies depending on the type of graphic that's selected:

- **Shape Format.** Appears when a shape is selected.

- **Picture Format.** Appears when a picture is selected.

- **Graphics Format.** Appears when an icon is selected.

You also can right-click a graphic and then choose its "Format" command (again, the name varies) at the bottom of the shortcut menu to open a pane with various formatting choices to the right of the worksheet. The formatting choices are so numerous that I can't cover them all, so this section touches on the basics.

To deselect one or more selected graphics, click away from the selection on the sheet.

Adding text to shapes

A shape on its own can look a little nondescript and may not communicate everything you need to communicate to your audience. For greater clarity, you can add text to a shape by following these steps:

1. **Double-click the shape or right-click it and choose Edit Text.** The blinking insertion point appears within the shape. For callout shapes, the insertion point appears in the shape automatically when you add it to the sheet.

2. **Type the text.** You can press Enter if you need to break the text into multiple lines after specific words; otherwise, Excel will wrap the text within the shape as needed.

3. **While you're adding the text, you can select it within the shape and use the choices in the Font group of the Home tab to change formatting.** I usually find that it's easier to use Shift plus the arrow keys to select text while working in a shape.

4. **Click outside the shape to finish.** In Figure 6.7, both the arrow and callout shapes have descriptive text added.

If you need to edit the shape's text, you can repeat Step 1. When editing, I tend to prefer to right-click the shape and choose Edit Text, because this selects all the text in the shape. In that situation, you can just start typing to replace all the text in the shape. Click outside the shape to finish.

	A	B	C	D	E	F	G	H
1	Sales Comparison							
2								
3	Location	2022	2023	$ Difference	% Difference			
4	N. Charlotte	$712,838.00	$708,914.00	-$3,924.00	99.45%			
5	S. Charlotte	674,998.00	462,434.00	-212,564.00	68.51%			
6	Winston-Salem	0.00	487,965.00	487,965.00	N/A		Highest	
7	Greensboro	493,046.00	677,701.00	184,655.00	137.45%		Percent	
8	Total	$1,882,904.00	$2,339,037.00	$456,133.00			Change!	
9								
10					Location			
11					opened in			
12					January.			
13								
14								

6.7 Shapes become more explanatory with added text.

Changing styles

The choices on the Shape Format, Picture Format, and Graphics Format tabs and the various formatting panes vary a bit, but generally they offer the ability to apply preset styles from the current theme. For shapes and icons, the Shape Styles and Graphics Styles groups hold both a gallery of preset styles you can apply, as well as fill, outline, and effects menus. As with other types of formatting, you can point to a choice in the gallery or menu to see a Live Preview, as in the example in Figure 6.8, and then click a choice to apply it to the selected object.

Genius

The Change Graphic button in the Change group at the far left in Figure 6.8 enables you to swap out one graphic for another. This works great if you've already formatted the graphic, because the new graphic will use the same formatting you applied to the previous one.

In addition to applying a style to a shape itself, the Shape Format tab includes a Word-Art Styles group with choices for styling the text within the shape. The Quick Styles gallery in the group offers preset WordArt styles with various combinations of text outlines, fills, and effects. Point to a style to see a Live Preview of its formatting on the text in the selected shape, and then click the preset to apply. The WordArt Styles group also includes Text Fill, Text Outline, and Text Effects choices for working with those individual aspects of styling text within a shape.

Caution

Applying some WordArt Quick Styles, such as a style that includes a heavy text outline and shading, can make small text far less readable, especially when the shape has a fill color. The same goes when you manually apply a text outline or effects. There's not a strict rule of thumb for how large the text should be, but I suggest increasing the text to 24 pts. or larger if you want to style it as WordArt.

Change Graphic button

Styles gallery

Graphics Format tab

Selected icon graphic showing Live Preview

6.8 It's easy to apply a preset style to a shape or icon, as well as to change the fill, outline, and effects.

The concept of "styles" works a bit differently on the Picture Format tab. The Picture Styles group holds a Quick Styles gallery, and its style choices are presets that change the picture "frame" or outline, as well as including other effects such as rotation and shadows. The Picture Styles group also has Picture Border and Picture Effects choices. What you may more think of as "styles" for pictures are collected in the Adjust group, in four galleries of presets:

- **Corrections.** Enables you to experiment with Sharpen/Soften and Brightness/Contrast variations.

- **Color.** Offers Color Saturation, Color Tone, and Recolor choices.

- **Artistic Effects.** Includes effects you can use to add interest to the picture, such as Paint Strokes and Crisscross Etching.

- **Transparency.** Holds presets for adjusting how see-through the image is.

Figure 6.9 shows the Picture Format tab where you can find all these choices. The figure also includes the Format Picture pane, with the Picture Color tools displayed. To get to those settings in the pane, you right-click a picture and choose Format Picture. Then click the Picture button at the top of the pane, and click Picture Color to expand its settings. You can leave the pane open as long as needed to move between and change settings and then click the pane Close (X) button to finish.

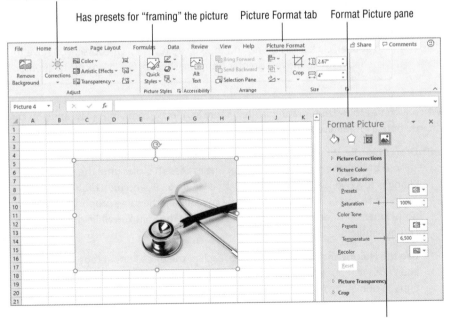

Has presets for changing the picture appearance

Has presets for "framing" the picture   Picture Format tab   Format Picture pane

Picture button

6.9 The Picture Format tab offers numerous types of presets.

If you've gone a little bit off the rails with too many picture format choices, select the picture and choose Picture Format → Adjust → Reset Picture.

Changing sizing and position

You learned earlier that a shape graphic appears where you drag on the sheet but that an inserted graphic sometimes appears near the active cell, whether or not that's where you need for it to be. The downloaded icon graphics generally have a standard 1 inch by 1 inch size, but the size for a downloaded picture might surprise you once it's on the sheet.

The fix for a misplaced graphic is pretty simple. Select it, and then use the mouse to drag it to another location. Also, by default, most graphics are set to move along with the cells nearby, should you insert or delete rows and columns in the sheet. If you want to turn this feature off, click the dialog box launcher for the Size group of the "Format" tab or click the Size & Properties button at the top if the "Format" pane is already open, click Properties in the pane to expand it, and click the Don't Move or Size with Cells option. (Note that the name of the tab and pane will vary depending on the type of graphic you've selected.)

To move a graphic to a sheet location that's not visible on-screen, you may prefer to cut and paste rather than dragging with the mouse. Cut the graphic (Ctrl+X), scroll to the approximate sheet location where you want the graphic to appear, click a cell there, and then paste (Ctrl+V). Of course, you have to cut and paste to move a graphic from one sheet or workbook file to another.

When it comes to resizing graphics, a few more subtleties come into play, and you can choose from a few different techniques:

- **Drag a handle.** White selection handles appear around the shape when it's selected. Move the mouse pointer over one of these handles until the pointer changes to a two-headed white arrow (see Figure 6.10), and then drag to the desired size and dimensions. If you want to maintain the same proportions in both dimensions (or aspect ratio), press and hold the Shift key while dragging a corner handle.

- **Use the Height and Width text boxes.** Each of the three Format tabs has Height and Width text boxes that you can use to adjust the graphic's size. Just select the entry in one of the text boxes, type a new entry, and press Enter. Or click the arrow buttons at the right end of each text box to change the size incrementally.

Apply WordArt Styles to shape text

Styles gallery Shape Format tab Height and Width text boxes

6.10 You can drag a resizing handle or use other methods to resize a graphic.

Resizing pointer   Additional settings

- **Use the "Format" pane.** If you click the dialog box launcher in the lower-right corner of the Size group, the "Format" pane (Format Shape in the case of Figure 6.10) opens and displays the Size settings. Not only can you adjust the Height and Width here, but you can also use the Scale Height or Scale Width choices to change the image size by a percentage. The Lock Aspect Ratio check box controls whether the graphic resizes proportionally in both dimensions. You can use the Reset button to return the picture to its original size. Close the pane when you've finished choosing resizing settings.

Caution

When using the Height and Width text boxes, keep in mind that the aspect ratio may or may not be locked, depending on the type of graphic. For example, the aspect ratio for shapes is generally not locked, so if you change the height, the width does not adjust, and this may distort the graphic. Pictures and icons, on the other hand, generally have a locked aspect ratio by default.

When you see a Crop button in the Size group of one of the "Format" tabs, it means you can crop out or eliminate part of the graphic that you don't want to show. Click that button, move the mouse pointer over the black border that appears until you see a black crop pointer, and then drag toward the middle of the graphic. Click outside the graphic or click the Crop button again to apply the crop. Cropping doesn't remove the cropped contents, it just hides them, so you can reset the picture or icon to redisplay the cropped portion under Size & Properties and then Size in the "Format" pane.

Working with layering, alignment, and rotation

There may be times when your design calls for multiple graphics, such as if you're combining multiple graphics to create something new or if you're using multiple icons to pump up your worksheet. Each of the "Format" tabs has an Arrange group, which offers the tools for positioning multiple graphics relative to one another in these two situations:

- **Layering.** Do you want the left half of the blue circle to be in front of or behind the right half of the red square where they overlap? You could select the blue circle and click the Bring Forward or Send Backward button. Each of those buttons also has a drop-down list arrow at the right that you can click so you can choose the Bring to Front or Send to Back command from the respective choices.

- **Aligning.** In cases where you want to align objects with more precision, select all the objects to align, and then click Align Objects in the Arrange group of the displayed "Format" tab. A menu of choices for aligning the objects horizontally or vertically relative to one another appears. For example, in Figure 6.11, I selected five inserted icons and then used Align Center to make sure they line up in a nice column. The commands in the menu are grouped. The first three control the horizontal alignment of the selected shapes, and the next three control the vertical alignment. The Distribute Horizontally command spaces graphics evenly between the far-left and far-right selected graphics, and Distribute Vertically spaces graphics evenly between the top and bottom selected graphics.

Genius

I use the Align Center and Align Middle choices a lot, because they create a uniform look even when the selected graphics have different sizes. And it's often the case that for a vertical arrangement of graphics like the one in Figure 6.11, I'll use Align Center and then Distribute Vertically for optimal alignment in both directions.

Rotation handle

Shapes aligned to their centers

6.11 Aligning objects relative to one another creates a neater layout.

You also can change the rotation of a graphic either to add interest or to fix a flaw. For example, if you inserted a digital photo that you took with your phone, it might look like it's "laying on its side" and needs to be rotated by 90 degrees. Changing the rotation is another instance where you can use various methods, depending on the degree of precision you need:

- **Use the rotation handle.** Figure 6.11 has a callout to a little doohickey called the *rotation handle*. When you move the mouse pointer over it, the pointer changes to a black version of the handle's circular arrow. At that point you can drag to the left or right to apply mild rotation, or you can drag diagonally for greater rotation. Yup, this is the least precise method.

- **Use the Rotate Objects presets.** The lower-right button in the Arrange group of the applicable "Format" tab is the Rotate Objects button. It has four presets for rotating a graphic: Rotate Right 90°, Rotate Left 90°, Flip Vertical, and Flip

Horizontal. The first two are the go-to fixes for badly rotated camera pictures, and the latter two are essentially 180-degree rotations. Each of these is a precise, easy rotation to apply.

- **Use the "Format" pane.** The last choice on the Rotate Objects menu is More Rotation Options. Choosing it opens the applicable "Format" pane to the Size settings shown in Figure 6.10. You can change the value in the Rotation text box to a precise rotation between 0 and 360 degrees. Close the pane after changing the setting. This, obviously, enables the most control over the rotation applied.

Note

In reality, 0 and 360 degrees are the same position, so if you still want a tiny amount of rotation, use a value less than 360 in the Rotation text box of the applicable "Format" pane. Also note that this text box allows you to enter values greater than 360, which then creates the question, "How many degrees of rotation have I really applied?" It seems easier to just stick with 0 to 359 as Rotation text box entries.

Inserting WordArt

During the earlier discussion about styling graphics, I explained how you can apply Word-Art styling to the text in a shape. You also can insert a standalone WordArt graphic object on a sheet. A WordArt object can be a more interesting replacement for a sheet title or could highlight an important point such as sale pricing. When you want to insert WordArt on the current sheet, follow these steps:

1. **Choose Insert → Text →WordArt.** The WordArt gallery shown in Figure 6.12 appears. To see a ScreenTip that describes the formatting for a gallery choice, move the mouse pointer over it. (Note that you also can insert other types of items such as text boxes using the choices in the Text group.)

2. **Click the desired WordArt preset in the gallery.** A WordArt object with selected *Your text here* placeholder text appears.

3. **Type your custom text for the WordArt graphic.** You can press the Enter key to insert hard line breaks, if needed.

4. **With the WordArt object still selected, use the choices on the Home and Shape Format tabs to adjust the WordArt formatting as desired.** In the example WordArt shown in Figure 6.12, I decreased the font size to 24 pt. so that the WordArt would fit in the space where the sheet title previously appeared.

5. **Click outside the WordArt to finish.**

Previously inserted, selected WordArt

Device	Watts	Hours Per Day	Watt-Hours Per Day
Lighting	100	9	900
Laptop	50	4	200
Computer monitor and tower	270	3	810
Inkjet printer	30	2	60
Phone charger	4	4	16

Business Energy Consumption

WordArt gallery

6.12 WordArt presets create a decorative text graphic on the worksheet.

You can edit the text within a WordArt graphic and change its formatting later as needed. Just click the WordArt object to select it and position the insertion point within its text. Make any desired edits and formatting changes, again using the choices on the Home and Shape Format tabs. For example, you can use the Shape Fill and Shape Outline choices in the Shape Styles group of the Shape Format tab to add a fill (outside of the text) and outline for the overall WordArt object. You also can resize the WordArt object, and when you do so, the text within rewraps as needed by default (unless, that is, you added hard line breaks when creating the WordArt). To access more detailed settings and choices for a selected WordArt graphic, right-click the WordArt object and click Format Shape to open the Format Shape pane. Click outside the graphic to deselect it.

Caution

Reformatting the text within a WordArt graphic can be a little wonky. Sometimes, changes apply with only the overall object selected. Sometimes, you have to drag over the text within the WordArt object for the formatting changes to apply, especially when you're changing the overall WordArt style using the Quick Styles gallery.

137

Combining and Creating Your Own Graphics

If you have time on your hands and want to experiment, you always can create your own logos, icons, and other graphics. Windows 10 of course includes the Paint and Paint 3-D apps for basic graphic editing, as well as the Snipping Tool and Snip & Sketch for capturing and annotating screenshots.

Beyond that, there are many free and low-cost tools out there for creating your own graphics. For example, GIMP (GNU Image Manipulation Program) is a free and open source program that lets you edit photos, create new images, and even create icons and other graphical elements. There are also specific free programs for creating vector graphics and icons, such as my favorite, Inkscape.

Note

Pictures are bitmap graphics composed of colored pixels, meaning they can lose sharpness when upsized. Vector graphics, in contrast, are defined by points, lines, and curves. Because vector graphics are essentially an outline or path, you can resize them without any loss in quality or sharpness. Shapes you insert in Excel are vector graphics. Icons are also vector graphics using the Scalable Vector Graphics (SVG) open standard for vector graphics. You also can insert a saved SVG graphic file on a worksheet.

Even if you don't want to spend time learning yet another program to create graphics, you can create your own custom graphics in Excel using a few little tricks I'm about to show you. Figure 6.13 shows a basic logo I created using just the tools in Excel.

Here's an overview of how I did it:

- **Create the parts.** I created a WordArt object, pressing Enter after typing 2Day so that the next line would align left evenly. I then inserted a separate Frame shape, dragging so that its center was approximately the same dimensions as the outer boundaries of the WordArt object.

Genius

Combining multiple graphics in Excel or other Microsoft 365 apps to create something completely different is an overlooked technique, in my opinion. For example, I like to use the Frame shape to create a custom frame around a picture, or overlap various shapes rather than trying to draw something freehand.

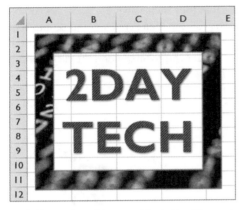

6.13 You can combine graphics in Excel to create a custom object.

- **Size and align the parts.** I then selected each object separately and used the mouse to further tweak the sizing to a more perfect fit. After that, I selected both objects using Shift+click and then chose Shape Format → Arrange → Align Objects → Align Center and Shape Format → Arrange → Align Objects → Align Middle to align the objects precisely.

- **Format the parts.** I first deselected the objects by clicking outside them and then reselected the Frame shape. I chose Shape Format → Shape Styles → Shape Fill → Picture. In the Insert Pictures window, I clicked Stock Images and chose an appropriate computer-y image to use as the fill for the frame. I then reselected the WordArt object, selected all its text, chose Shape Format → WordArt Styles → Quick Styles, and chose another style that better matched the Frame shape's image fill. I could have taken it even further and added a fill for the WordArt background, but I thought that would be too much.

- **Group the parts.** After Shift+clicking each shape, I chose Shape Format → Arrange → Group Objects → Group. (I could later use the Ungroup choice to convert the Frame shape and WordArt back to separate graphics, if needed.)

Caution

Grouping temporarily combines multiple separate objects into a single object that you can select, move, and copy as a single unit. However, when it comes to resizing or reformatting a grouped object, you can get some unexpected results. For example, if I dragged a corner handle to resize my Figure 6.13 logo, the WordArt didn't resize correctly with the frame. And If I tried to add a shape outline, the outline appeared around both the objects.

Another cool thing about the stock icons is that they themselves are generally combinations of multiple vector shapes. This means you can break an icon graphic into separate pieces to format the pieces individually. To break apart an icon, either select the icon and choose Graphics Format → Change → Convert to Shape or right-click the icon and choose Convert to Shape. After that, try choosing Shape Format → Arrange → Group Objects → Ungroup to see whether the object breaks down into even more pieces that you can format individually. For example, in Figure 6.14, I converted and ungrouped a fluorescent bulb icon and then changed the fill for one of its pieces to a lighter color. I could add a frame or thick box around it and regroup everything to create an icon with a new look.

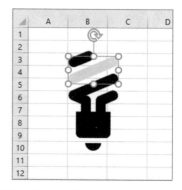

6.14 Breaking apart an icon and reformatting its parts presents another opportunity to go custom.

Saving Your Custom Graphic

Here's where we enter double-extra bonus territory. You can save a custom graphic that you've created and grouped as a separate graphic file that you can use over and over. Here's how to do it, using the Windows Paint program in the process. (You could use another graphics program that you prefer, too.) Select the grouped object and choose Home → Clipboard. Then click the drop-down list arrow at the right side of the Copy button and choose Copy as Picture. In the Copy Picture dialog box that appears, I usually leave the default As Shown on Screen option selected but change Format to Bitmap and then click OK. (If you don't choose Bitmap, any text may look raggedy when pasted.) Then, start Paint using either the Start menu or the Search box on the Windows taskbar. Choose Home → Clipboard → Paste. The pasted area should be selected by default, but if it isn't, choose Home → Image → Select (the top part of button) and drag to reselect the pasted area. Then immediately choose Home

➔ Image ➔ Crop or press Ctrl+Shift+X to crop out any excess. You can then choose File ➔ Save and use the Save As dialog box to save in the desired location and format. Granted, bitmap images are a little less flexible than vector graphics, but having a custom graphic available for reuse in other files can help you with design consistency and branding.

Creating and Working with SmartArt

As if the preceding array of graphics types wasn't enough, like many of its Microsoft 365 peers, Excel enables you to create a special type of diagram called *SmartArt*. SmartArt automatically adds a predesigned shape to illustrate each text item you add, so you don't have to draw individual shapes, insert text, line up the shapes, and so on, to create a comprehensive graphic. You can create a SmartArt graphic to diagram a list, process, cycle, hierarchy or org chart, and many other types of relationships. Some SmartArt formats even enable you to insert pictures. The possibilities are endless, so this section covers the essentials with a simple example or two in the figures.

Adding a SmartArt graphic

The initial steps for adding a SmartArt graphic are fairly consistent. To insert SmartArt on the current sheet, follow these steps:

1. **Choose Insert ➔ Illustrations ➔ SmartArt.** The Choose a SmartArt Graphic dialog box appears.

2. **Choose a category in the list at the left, and then click a thumbnail in the middle section.** A preview and description of the selected diagram type appears at the right, as shown in Figure 6.15. You can continue browsing the formats by changing categories and thumbnails until you find a format you think will work.

Note The SmartArt Design ➔ Create Graphic ➔ Text Pane button toggles Text pane display on and off, so choose that button if you don't see the pane. The pane also disappears when the SmartArt graphic isn't selected, and clicking back in a shape with the [Text] prompt reselects the SmartArt.

3. **With the desired category and thumbnail selected, click OK.** The initial shape appears with placeholder text. By default, a Text pane with *Type Your Text Here* at the top appears beside the graphic.

Choose a SmartArt Graphic   ?   ✕

- All
- List
- **Process**
- Cycle
- Hierarchy
- Relationship
- Matrix
- Pyramid
- Picture
- Office.com

Basic Chevron Process

Use to show a progression; a timeline; sequential steps in a task, process, or workflow; or to emphasize movement or direction. Level 1 text appears inside an arrow shape while Level 2 text appears below the arrow shapes.

OK   Cancel

6.15 Preview the SmartArt diagram type before inserting the graphic.

4. **Type the text for each shape on a separate bullet line in the Text pane.** You can use the down arrow key to move down from one line to the next for the initial three bullets. After that, you can press Enter to add more bullets (and individual shapes in the graphic). Figure 6.16 shows the first two items in a list of data entered for a SmartArt graphic and the resulting shapes. (Most SmartArt graphics list more items. I chose to show an "in-process" list so the text in the shapes would be legible in the figure. You can see that the third bullet line in the Text pane has a [Text] place-holder for the third shape, awaiting the next entry.) Some SmartArt formats have indented sub-bullets below the main level bullets. Press Tab to indent a bullet and convert it to a sub-bullet. Optionally, you can click a shape in the diagram and type its contents.

5. **Drag the graphic to a new location and resize it as needed.** For example, you could drag the graphic to the left side of an empty sheet and drag a corner selec-tion handle to resize it to a larger size that makes the text more readable.

6. **Click outside the graphic to finish.**

Caution

SmartArt graphics can be pretty big, so sometimes it makes sense to place one on a sheet by itself; create, size, and position it as desired; and then add supporting data in the nearby cells.

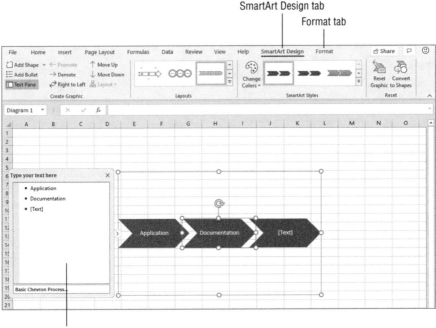

SmartArt Design tab

Format tab

Text pane

6.16 Enter the text for each SmartArt shape in the Text pane.

Some types of SmartArt graphics have an additional step to complete before Step 5: adding the pictures. For layouts requiring pictures, the Text pane and/or shapes include a button you can click to insert a picture. The Insert Pictures dialog box that appears enables you to choose whether to insert a file, stock image, online picture, or icon.

Editing and rearranging shapes

You can use the choices in the Create Graphic group of the SmartArt Design tab to work with the shapes in the graphic. The choices that are active there depend on the SmartArt graphic type and the currently selected shape. For example, as shown in Figure 6.17, when you select a lower-level shape in an organization chart diagram (found within the Hierarchy category), nearly all of the choices in the Create Graphic group become active and available.

Choices for working with shapes

The Create Graphic group holds the choices for working with the shapes in a SmartArt graphic. *(Figure 6.17 — toolbar/ribbon and worksheet screenshot)*

Selected shape

6.17 The Create Graphic group holds the choices for working with the shapes in a SmartArt graphic.

Again, covering all the possibilities of how every choice works in every graphic type and shape position would involve more pages than we're able to spend together, so experiment at your leisure. I'll highlight the Add Shape choice, which you can use to add a shape into the diagram if you're not comfortable doing it via the Text pane, and the Layout button, which you can use to change the arrangement of the shapes for some SmartArt diagrams.

Genius

You often don't need the assistant shape that's just below and to the left of the top level of an organization chart graphic, as in the example in Figure 6.17. Here's the trick for deleting it. Select the SmartArt graphic, click the assistant shape in the graphic, and then click the selection border *again* to make sure that the shape is really selected. Then press the Delete key.

Changing the graphic type and formatting

To change the overall layout and style for a selected SmartArt graphic, you can use the SmartArt Styles and Layouts galleries in the groups of those names on the SmartArt Design tab, as shown in Figure 6.17. Changing the applied style can really change the look of the graphic, as SmartArt Styles often are more three-dimensional than styles for other types of graphics such as shapes. The SmartArt Styles group also includes the Change Colors button, which opens to a gallery of alternate color combinations, based on the theme applied to the workbook file, that you can apply to the graphic.

The name of the Layouts gallery is a little misleading, because the choices here basically change to another overall SmartArt design. You can even click More Layouts at the bottom of the gallery to go all the way back to the Choose a SmartArt Graphic dialog box.

The Format tab (refer to Figure 6.16) offers choices more tailored to formatting an individual shape that you've selected by clicking it within the overall SmartArt graphic. The Change Shape choice in the Shapes group enables you to change the Shape of the selected item, while the Shape Styles group holds the choices for restyling the selected shape.

Note

Based on my escapades with formatting SmartArt graphics over the years, it seems like changing the Theme Effects has the greatest impact on SmartArt Styles. You can give it a try, too, by making another Page Layout → Themes →Effects choice and then previewing the Shape Styles on a selected Smart-Art graphic.

Deleting a Graphic

To delete a graphic of any type, click it so that selection handles appear around it, and then press the Delete key. Use caution when you do this, however, because Excel doesn't give you any warning before zapping away your lovely graphic. If you need the graphic back, press Ctrl+Z or click the Undo button on the QAT immediately to undo the deletion.

You can keep graphics you've created handy for later use by collecting them on a separate sheet in the workbook file. Add a new, blank sheet, and then change its name to something like Graphics or Scrap. Then, when you no longer want a graphic, cut it and paste it to the Graphics or Scrap sheet. Then, you'll still have it around if you need to use it or create a variation of it for another sheet or workbook file.

Genius

Each of the Format tabs also has a Selection Pane button in the Arrange group. Clicking this button opens the Selection pane, where you can select a graphic by clicking its name. The more useful feature of this pane is that you can click the eye icon to the right of any listed graphic to toggle display of the graphic on and off. If you think you might want to use a graphic later, you can hide it rather than deleting it.

Adding a Background Image

You can accomplish a much less frequent choice for adding graphics to a sheet—adding a background image—using the Page Layout → Page Setup → Background choice, which opens the Insert Pictures window shown in Figure 6.18. Use the choices here to navigate to and select or search for an image to insert.

		✕
Insert Pictures		☺ ☹
🖳 From a file	Browse ▸	
🅱 Bing Image Search	Search Bing 🔎	
☁ OneDrive - Personal	Browse ▸	

6.18 Use the choices here to insert a sheet background graphic.

Three important caveats apply for background pictures. First, Excel tiles or repeats the picture to fill the sheet. This might result in a too-busy appearance that inhibits readability. Next, if the picture is very dark or very light, there might not be enough contrast between the background and the font color. (Most experts say that dark text on a light background is most readable.) Finally, background images only display and don't print. So, their use works best when you want to pretty up a sheet in a workbook that's primarily used for data input by other users.

Note
You can add a background image that appears on every page, such as an organization logo, but you have to do that as part of a header or footer. The Chapter 9 section called "Creating Headers and Footers" covers this technique, which is another way to add a graphic and bolster brand identity on a sheet.

146

How Do I Manage Lists of Information?

	A	B	C	D	E	F	G	H
1	Dinnerware Stock							
2								
3	ID ▼	Item ▼	Pattern ▼	Size (in.) ▼	Cost ▼	Retail Price ▼	# in Stock ▼	Inventory Cost ▼
4	1	Cup	Lily	3	2.50	5.00	73	182.50
5	2	Cereal Bowl	Rose	6	6.00	10.00	112	672.00
6	3	Saucer	Rose	6	1.50	3.00	88	132.00
7	4	Dinner Plate	Sunflower	10.5	10.00	20.00	51	510.00
8	5	Saucer	Sunflower	6	1.50	3.00	69	103.50
9	6	Soup Bowl	Lily	8	10.00	20.00	37	370.00
10	7	Salad Plate	Rose	8	4.25	8.50	115	488.75
11	8	Cup	Rose	3	2.50	5.00	144	360.00
12	9	Cereal Bowl	Lily	6	6.00	10.00	30	180.00
13	10	Saucer	Lily	6	1.50	3.00	133	199.50
14	11	Salad Plate	Sunflower	8	4.25	8.50	151	641.75
15	12	Soup Bowl	Sunflower	8	None	20.00	88	880.00
16	13	Soup Bowl	Rose	8	Average	20.00	91	910.00
17	14	Cereal Bowl	Sunflower	6	Count Count Number	10.00	58	348.00
18	15	Salad Plate	Lily	8	Max Min	8.50	131	556.75
19	16	Dinner Plate	Rose	10.5	Sum	20.00	111	1110.00
20	17	Cup	Sunflower	3	StdDev Var	5.00	103	257.50
21	18	Dinner Plate	Lily	10.5	More Function	20.00	100	1000.00
22	Total				▼			8902.25
23								

Many organizations and individuals live and die by their lists. Lists of products. Lists of employees. Home inventory insurance lists. To-do lists. Excel excels at helping users track lists in neat rows and columns. It can help you build a list with Flash Fill. You can sort and filter list contents with ease. Convert a list to a table for easier styling, sorting, filtering, and calculating. If you no longer need the fancy features, convert the table back to a regular list. This chapter shares all of these list skills so you can run your lists like a boss.

Arranging a List in Excel

Excel can function as a simple database, enabling you to use the Data tab to perform common but powerful business tasks such as sorting and filtering the list. There's a catch, as usual. You have to arrange the data correctly so that Excel's data management tools can recognize the list. Good list setup requires following just a few straightforward rules:

- **The list should be in a contiguous range.** Any blank column or row would essentially split the table, though it's usually okay to have a few blank cells here and there within a list.

- **There should be at least one blank row above the table and one blank column to the right.** This is essentially the opposite of the first rule. It's important because if you do sort or filter the table, that could also change the location or position of any cell touching the list whether you want that or not.

- **There generally should be a row at the top of the table with the label for each column of information.** In database lingo, these are called *field names*, where each column holds a separate field or type of information. Various dialog boxes in Excel also call these *headers*, or a *header row*, which are separate from the sheet headers with row numbers and column letters.

- **Each column should hold a single type of information.** A column should hold all text entries, all currency, all dates, and so on.

- **Each column should hold a discrete piece of data to facilitate sorting and filtering.** The classic example of flubbing this rule is putting both a first and last name in the same field or column. The first name should be one column and the last name another column; otherwise, you wouldn't be able to sort the list by last name. Similarly, you wouldn't want to include a product's size or color in the same cell with the product name. When in doubt, break it out (to its own field).

- **Each complete list entry should occupy a single row.** One person's contact information should be in a single row, the details about one product should be in a single row, and so on. Database folks call each row entry a *record*.

Some of the figures in earlier chapters showed simple lists of data, so I developed a more robust example for Figure 7.1.

Blank row above list

Headers for each column of
data in the list in row 3

▲	A	B	C	D	E	F	G
1	Dinnerware Stock						
2							
3	Item	Pattern	Size (in.)	Cost	Retail Price	# in Stock	
4	Cup	Lily	3	2.50	5.00	73	
5	Cereal Bowl	Rose	6	6.00	10.00	112	
6	Saucer	Rose	6	1.50	3.00	88	
7	Dinner Plate	Sunflower	10.5	10.00	20.00	51	
8	Saucer	Sunflower	6	1.50	3.00	69	
9	Soup Bowl	Lily	8	10.00	20.00	37	
10	Salad Plate	Rose	8	4.25	8.50	115	
11	Cup	Rose	3	2.50	5.00	144	
12	Cereal Bowl	Lily	6	6.00	10.00	30	
13	Saucer	Lily	6	1.50	3.00	133	
14	Salad Plate	Sunflower	8	4.25	8.50	151	
15	Soup Bowl	Sunflower	8	10.00	20.00	88	
16	Soup Bowl	Rose	8	10.00	20.00	91	
17	Cereal Bowl	Sunflower	6	6.00	10.00	58	
18	Salad Plate	Lily	8	4.25	8.50	131	
19	Dinner Plate	Rose	10.5	10.00	20.00	111	
20	Cup	Sunflower	3	2.50	5.00	103	
21	Dinner Plate	Lily	10.5	10.00	20.00	100	
22							
23							

List in range A3:F21

Blank column to the
right of list

Complete entry in each row

7.1 A list of data occupies a contiguous range.

Excel includes some special shortcut key combinations for moving within the contiguous table range and making selections within the table range. These can be especially important to know if you have a long list of data, such as data you've imported from a database or other source. Give these shortcut key combos a try in your lists:

- **Ctrl+up arrow or Ctrl+down arrow.** Pressing one of these keyboard shortcuts moves to the top or bottom row of the table, within the current column. When the active cell is in a column outside a table, these shortcuts move to the top or bottom row of the sheet instead. (Though if you're working below the table, the first time you press Ctrl+up arrow, it moves to the bottom row of the table.)

- **Ctrl+left arrow or Ctrl+right arrow.** Pressing one of these keyboard shortcuts moves to the far-left or far-right column of the table, within the current row. When the active cell is in a row below or above the table, these shortcuts move to the far-left or far-right column of the sheet. (If you're working to the right of the table, the first time you press Ctrl+left arrow, it moves to the far-right column of the table.)

- **Ctrl+Shift+arrow.** This keyboard combination makes a selection in the direction of the arrow key that you press, starting from the active cell and stopping at the edge of the table. Outside of a table, Ctrl+Shift+right arrow selects the row from the active cell through the rightmost column of the sheet, while Ctrl+Shift+down arrow selects the column from the active cell down to the last row in the sheet.

- **Ctrl+Shift+* (asterisk).** This keyboard combo selects the entire table as well as any other contiguous range.

Cleaning Up Data

If you weren't the person who created the workbook file with one or more lists of data, you might find that the lists aren't set up correctly. Or, the data may have been exported from another source that breaks up the data differently than you'd like. Don't start tearing your hair out just yet! The Data tab offers tools for performing a variety of data cleanup operations. This section covers these time-savers.

Genius

You can use data validation to prevent entries of the wrong type in a list or table column. Select a column range, and then choose Data → Data Tools → Data Validation (left side of button). Use the Allow drop-down list to specify a type of validation to apply, such as Whole Number or Date. Specify other settings (choices vary depending on the validation type), and click OK. The range will then only accept entries that match the validation criteria.

Using Flash Fill

Flash Fill is a special kind of fill that combines the entries from two or more columns into a single entry in a new column. Once again, first and last names serve as the most common example. So, *John* in the FirstName column and *Smith* in the LastName column could be combined as *John Smith* in a new column. Another way you could use this feature would be to combine a product name from one column with other descriptive information in the next column, to create a more descriptive name in a new column that you could then copy to another document.

As when filling a series of numbers, a technique that Chapter 2 covered, you have to establish the pattern that Flash Fill should use to combine the entries into a new column. These steps show you how it's done:

1. **Select the cell at the top of the column to the right of the columns to combine.**

2. **Type the combined entry and press Enter.** In the example in Figure 7.2, I've typed the entries from columns A and B, separated by a , (comma) into column C. That's right, you can even add simple punctuation when you use Flash Fill, such as adding periods when combining entries from a column that holds middle initials. Optionally, you could also reselect the cell holding your pattern entry at the top of the column; Flash Fill works when either that cell or the cell below it is selected.

7.2 The entry you make at the top of the column establishes the pattern for Flash Fill.

3. **Choose Data → Data Tools → Flash Fill or press Ctrl+E.** The Flash Fill feature combines and fills the entries down the column, as in the resulting example shown in Figure 7.3. If the Flash Fill button is grayed out or inactive, that means the pattern example you entered in Step 2 won't work, so try another variation.

153

	A	B	C
1	Item	Pattern	Ship Name
2	Cup	Lily	Cup, Lily
3	Cereal Bowl	Rose	Cereal Bowl, Rose
4	Saucer	Rose	Saucer, Rose
5	Dinner Plate	Sunflower	Dinner Plate, Sunflower
6	Saucer	Sunflower	Saucer, Sunflower
7	Soup Bowl	Lily	Soup Bowl, Lily
8	Salad Plate	Rose	Salad Plate, Rose
9	Cup	Rose	Cup, Rose
10	Cereal Bowl	Lily	Cereal Bowl, Lily
11	Saucer	Lily	Saucer, Lily
12	Salad Plate	Sunflower	Salad Plate, Sunflower
13	Soup Bowl	Sunflower	Soup Bowl, Sunflower
14	Soup Bowl	Rose	Soup Bowl, Rose
15	Cereal Bowl	Sunflower	Cereal Bowl, Sunflower
16	Salad Plate	Lily	Salad Plate, Lily
17	Dinner Plate	Rose	Dinner Plate, Rose
18	Cup	Sunflower	Cup, Sunflower
19	Dinner Plate	Lily	Dinner Plate, Lily
20			

7.3 Flash Fill finishes the column of combined entries.

Note Rather than the previous Step 3, you could begin typing the second entry in the column to Flash Fill. When Excel recognizes the pattern and previews the rest of the entries to be filled, press Enter to accept the filled entries.

In some cases, Flash Fill also can be used to separate entries from a column of cells. To accomplish that, you use separate columns to hold the reverse-engineered pattern examples. In a case where a single column holds first and last names combined, as in *John Smith*, you would enter *John* in the next column to the right and *Smith* in the column to the right of that. Then use the Flash Fill button or Ctrl+E for each column to fill the separated parts of the original entries.

Caution When you use Flash Fill to separate entries, it works best when all the entries have the same number of words or items in the cell. For example, if some cells have two words and others have three, Flash Fill might drop the middle word and just fill the first and third words.

Using Text to Columns

In addition to copying or importing data from another file, you might obtain the data for your list from any number of other sources. You might have copied information from a company web page or scanned a hard-copy document and converted it to text using optical character recognition (OCR) software. Transitions like these can result in column entries that combine the data in unexpected ways.

The Text to Columns feature gives you the power to separate text in a column when the entries have more complicated patterns. It can divide data from a single column into multiple separate columns when the data entries use one of these methods or patterns:

- **Delimited.** This means that a special character separates each item or field that you want to break into a separate column, such as a comma or semicolon. The special character, also called a *delimiter*, enables Text to Columns to automatically identify how to break apart the source entries.

- **Fixed width.** This means that the entries to break apart are roughly the same width with spaces in between, as if they are in columns within the original column. In other words, you can see where you can neatly break the source column data into multiple separate columns and specify those breaks.

Follow these steps when you need to give the Text to Columns feature a try for a column holding delimited data:

1. **In the source column, select the range of cells holding the data you want to separate.**

2. **Choose Data → Data Tools → Text to Columns.** (Refer to Figure 7.2.) The Convert Text to Columns Wizard dialog box appears.

3. **Leave the Delimited option selected or click Fixed Width, and then click Next.** The next wizard dialog box appears.

4. **The next action at this point varies depending on whether you selected Delimited or Fixed Width in Step 3:**

   - **Under Delimiters, click to check the desired delimiter and uncheck unneeded delimiters.** For example, in Figure 7.4, I've checked the Comma delimiter and have unchecked the others, though you can select multiple delimiters. To specify a different delimiter character, click the Other check box to check it, and then type the delimiter into the accompanying text box. The Data Preview area at the bottom of the dialog box shows you how the separated entries will look. The listed city names made the column A data too complicated to separate using Flash Fill or a formula, given that there are one- and two-word names, and one name even includes a period.

Delimiter

Entries to separate   Preview of separated data

7.4 Check the Data Preview carefully when specifying delimiters.

- **Click on the ruler at the top of the Data Preview to insert breaks between the aligned columns of fixed width data.** You also can drag a break line to move it or double-click a break line to delete it.

5. **Click Next.** The final wizard dialog box appears, offering the ability for you to change the data type or format for one or more columns. Optionally, you can click Finish in this step instead of Next, if you know you don't want to change any column data types.

6. **To change a column's data format, click the column in the Data Preview area, and then click an option under Column Data Format.** The Data Preview has scroll bars so you can scroll other columns into view, if needed. The available data formats are General, Text, and Date. You can click the Advanced button to specify the decimal separator and other number formatting and then click OK. You also can use the Destination box to specify another output column on the sheet for the contents of the selected preview columns.

7. **Click Finish.** The separated data is placed in one or more columns to the right of the source column cells you selected in Step 1. Figure 7.5 shows how the data selected in Figure 7.4 looked after I used Text to Columns to separate the data into separate City and State columns.

Caution   If there is any data in the cells where Text to Columns needs to place its results, a message box appears, asking if you want to replace the data. Click OK to do so or Cancel to stop the Text to Columns process and leave the data intact. You can then move the range of data that needs to be separated into columns to another location before trying Text to Columns again.

Removing duplicates and consolidating

Sometimes a list of data that you've inherited from another source has other problems that can either skew the results when you try to analyze the data or just make the data plain impossible to work with. The Data Tools group of the Data tab has a couple more tricks up its sleeve to help you in these jams.

Consider a list that tracks parts for a manufacturing operation, including the value of the parts on hand and reorder quantities. What if one or more of the row entries somehow gets duplicated? This would cause the total inventory value to be wrong and perhaps cause reordering errors. Excel can help you find and remove duplicate entries, using these steps:

	A	B
1	City	State
2	Toledo	OH
3	Baton Rouge	LA
4	St. Louis	MO
5	New York	NY
6	Kansas City	MO
7	Durham	NC
8		

7.5 Text to Columns separated data into City and State columns.

1. **Select the list range that may have the duplicate entries.**

2. **Choose Data → Data Tools → Remove Duplicates.** (Refer to Figure 7.2.) The Remove Duplicates dialog box shown in Figure 7.6 appears.

3. **Under Columns, click to clear the check box beside any column that you don't want to check.**

4. **Click OK.** A message box appears to tell you how many duplicates were removed and how many unique entries remain. Or, if there were no duplicates, an alternate message box informs you of that.

5. **Click OK again to close the message box.**

Remove Duplicates

To delete duplicate values, select one or more columns that contain duplicates.

Select All | Unselect All | ☑ My data has headers

Columns
☑ City
☑ State

OK | Cancel

7.6 If needed, deselect one or more columns when removing duplicates.

Genius

You can limit entries in selected cells by creating a pick (drop-down) list. First, enter the list items in an out-of-sight area on the current sheet or on another sheet. Select the column range where you want the cells to have a list. Choose Data → Data Tools → Data Validation (main part of button). Choose List from the Allow drop-down list, use the Source box to select the range where you entered the list items, and then click OK.

If someone created a sheet with small areas of similar data that you need to work with as a whole, you can consolidate the data into a single range. You'll get what I mean as you walk through the steps for this process, with my explanation of the accompanying example:

1. **Select the upper-left cell in the range where you want to output the consolidated data.** Of course, you want to make sure there are enough blank cells below and to the right of the selected cell to hold the data.

2. **Choose Data → Data Tools → Consolidate.** (Refer to Figure 7.2.) The Consolidate dialog box shown in Figure 7.7 appears, although if you're just starting to consolidate the data, the All References list would be empty.

3. **Use the Reference text box to select a range to consolidate.** To do this, use the collapse button at the right end of the box, use the mouse to select the range on the active sheet or another sheet, and then click the expand button at the right end of the box.

4. **Click Add to add the selected reference to the All References list.**

Consolidated result

Four ranges to consolidate

7.7 Consolidating data lists it together or creates a summary.

5. **Repeat Steps 3 and 4 as needed to include additional ranges to consolidate.**

6. **Under Use Labels In, click the Top Row and Left Column check boxes as needed.** This specifies whether the labels will be used in the consolidated range.

7. **Click OK.**

If identical ranges to consolidate are on different sheets, the Function choice at the top of the Consolidate dialog box comes into play. In that case, the Consolidate feature doesn't compile a list from all the source ranges; it instead uses the calculation specified by the Function choice to summarize the data, typically on a separate sheet. So, the Sum function would total the data in the consolidated summary range. In this kind of arrangement, you might also click the Create Links to Source Data check box to check it so that changes to the values or formulas in the source sheets are reflected in the summary calculation.

Sorting, Filtering, and Subtotaling Lists of Information

Breaking your lists into discrete fields of information makes the data more usable, because it means you can sort and filter the list. These two forms of basic data analysis help you find more meaning in the list. You can arrange the list contents in a more meaningful way, such as sorting by customer or order number. Or, you can limit the list to just the items that are relevant for a particular purpose.

Sorting and filtering a list

As the name says, *sorting* rearranges the entries (rows) in a list into a new order. Placing entries in alphabetical order (A to Z or Z to A) always comes to mind, but Excel also can sort by number (Smallest to Largest or Largest to Smallest) and date (Newest to Oldest or Oldest to Newest).

The quickest way to sort according to the contents of a single column is to click a cell in the column and then choose either Data ➔ Sort & Filter ➔ Sort A to Z or Data ➔ Sort & Filter ➔ Sort Z to A.

Note

In the olden days, when you sorted any list in Excel, the entire worksheet rows moved. This was a problem if you had other ranges of data to the right of the list or table. Now, Excel only changes the order of the rows in the list or table. This is why you need to leave one or more blank columns to the right of the list or table. If you don't, nonlist data touching the list gets sorted, too.

Follow these steps to sort data by two or more columns, sometimes called a *multilevel sort*:

1. **Click in the list you want to sort.**

2. **Choose Data ➔ Sort & Filter ➔ Sort.** The Sort dialog box appears, and Excel selects the table on the sheet.

3. **In the first Sort By row, choose the column to sort by from the Sort By drop-down list.**

4. **Choose the sort order from the Order drop-down list.** You optionally can use the Sort On list to choose to sort according to certain formatting settings rather than the cell values.

5. **Click the Add Level button.** This adds a Then By level below the Sort By level.

6. **Repeat the techniques presented in Steps 3 and 4 to specify sort settings for the Then By row.** From here, you could optionally repeat the previous step and this one to add sort levels.

7. **Make sure that My Data Has Headers is checked if that is true of your list.**

8. **Click OK.**

Figure 7.8 shows the Sort dialog box with settings for two sort levels applied, as well as the resulting sort in the table. I sorted first by the Pattern column in A to Z order and second by Cost from Largest to Smallest. Press Ctrl+Z to undo the sort before saving the file.

Data sorted first by Pattern

Sort buttons   Filter buttons

	A	B	C	D	E	F	G	H
1	Dinnerware Stock							
2								
3	ID	Item	Pattern	Size (in.)	Cost			
4	6	Soup Bowl	Lily	8	10.00			
5	18	Dinner Plate	Lily	10.5	10.00			
6	9	Cereal Bowl	Lily	6	6.00			
7	15	Salad Plate	Lily	8	4.25			
8	1	Cup	Lily	3	2.50			
9	10	Saucer	Lily	6	1.50			
10	13	Soup Bowl	Rose	8	10.00			
11	16	Dinner Plate	Rose	10.5	10.00			
12	2	Cereal Bowl	Rose	6	6.00			
13	7	Salad Plate	Rose	8	4.25	8.50	115	
14	8	Cup	Rose	3	2.50	5.00	144	
15	3	Saucer	Rose	6	1.50	3.00	88	
16	4	Dinner Plate	Sunflower	10.5	10.00	20.00	51	
17	12	Soup Bowl	Sunflower	8	10.00	20.00	88	
18	14	Cereal Bowl	Sunflower	6	6.00	10.00	58	
19	11	Salad Plate	Sunflower	8	4.25	8.50	151	
20	17	Cup	Sunflower	3	2.50	5.00	103	
21	5	Saucer	Sunflower	6	1.50	3.00	69	
22								

Then sorted by Cost

7.8 Use the Sort dialog box to sort by multiple columns.

Genius

In the sheet shown in Figure 7.8, I added a column with numbers at the far left to number the items in their original order. You can do this in a list that you might sort a lot but need to be able to return it to its original order. Even if you hide that column from view, you can still sort by it.

Filtering doesn't change the list order. It just temporarily hides some of the rows so you can focus on relevant information. Filtering is just as easy as sorting. Start by choosing Data → Sort & Filter → Filter. This displays a filter arrow to the right of each column name in the header row. Click the filter arrow for a column to filter by, and in the menu/dialog

161

box that appears, click the (Select All) check box to clear it. Click to place a check in the check box for each entry in that column that you want to display in the filtered data, and then click OK. Repeat the process for other columns to further filter and narrow the list of matches. Figure 7.9 shows a list filtered to only show rows with Lily in the Pattern column. Notice that the filter arrow for a filtered column changes to include a little filter icon. The row numbers for the filtered rows also change to blue.

Indicates a filtered column   Filter arrow

⊿	A	B	C	D	E	F	G	H
1		Dinnerware Stock						
2								
3	⌄	Item ⌄	Patter ⌄	Size (in ⌄	Cost ⌄	Retail Price ⌄	# in Sto ⌄	
4	1	Cup	Lily	3	2.50	5.00	73	
9	6	Soup Bowl	Lily	8	10.00	20.00	37	
12	9	Cereal Bowl	Lily	6	6.00	10.00	30	
13	10	Saucer	Lily	6	1.50	3.00	133	
18	15	Salad Plate	Lily	8	4.25	8.50	131	
21	18	Dinner Plate	Lily	10.5	10.00	20.00	100	
22								

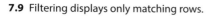

Filtered for rows with Lily

7.9 Filtering displays only matching rows.

To remove a filter from a column, you can click its filter arrow, click the (Select All) check box to recheck it, and then click OK. To clear filters from all columns, choose Data → Sort & Filter → Clear. You can then choose Data → Sort & Filter → Filter to toggle off the filter arrows.

Subtotaling a sorted list

After a list has been sorted, you can add subtotals to summarize data in one or more columns. This simultaneously applies outlining that you can use to expand and collapse the data to further zero in on a pertinent subset of information.

Click a cell in the sorted list, and then choose Data → Outline → Subtotal to open the Subtotal dialog box. From the At Each Change In list, choose a sorted field that corresponds to each subset of data that you want to subtotal. Choose another function from the Use Function list, if needed. Then, in the Add Subtotal To list, click to check the check box for each field for which you want to display a subtotal. Click OK to apply the subtotals.

Notice in Figure 7.10 that outlining buttons and levels appear to the left of the sheet. For example, you can click the - (minus) button to collapse that level of the outline. The subtotals and outlining remain applied until you remove them by clicking the Remove All button back in the Subtotal dialog box.

Field that determines each data subset

		A	B	C	D	E	F	G	H	I	J	K	L
1		Dinnerware Stock								Subtotal	?	×	
2										At each change in:			
3		ID	Item	Pattern	Size (in.)	Cost	Retail Price	# in Stock		Pattern		∨	
4		6	Soup Bowl	Lily	8	10.00	20.00	37		Use function:			
5		18	Dinner Plate	Lily	10.5	10.00	20.00	100		Sum		∨	
6		9	Cereal Bowl	Lily	6	6.00	10.00	30		Add subtotal to:			
7		15	Salad Plate	Lily	8	4.25	8.50	131		☐ Item			
8		1	Cup	Lily	3	2.50	5.00	73		☐ Pattern			
9		10	Saucer	Lily	6	1.50	3.00	133		☐ Size (in.)			
10				Lily Total				504		☐ Cost ☐ Retail Price ☑ # in Stock			
11		13	Soup Bowl	Rose	8	10.00	20.00	91					
12		16	Dinner Plate	Rose	10.5	10.00	20.00	111		☑ Replace current subtotals			
13		2	Cereal Bowl	Rose	6	6.00	10.00	112		☐ Page break between groups			
14		7	Salad Plate	Rose	8	4.25	8.50	115		☑ Summary below data			
15		8	Cup	Rose	3	2.50	5.00	144		Remove All	OK	Cancel	
16		3	Saucer	Rose	6	1.50	3.00	88					
17				Rose Total				661					
18		4	Dinner Plate	Sunflower	10.5	10.00	20.00	51					
19		12	Soup Bowl	Sunflower	8	10.00	20.00	88					
20		14	Cereal Bowl	Sunflower	6	6.00	10.00	58					
21		11	Salad Plate	Sunflower	8	4.25	8.50	151					
22		17	Cup	Sunflower	3	2.50	5.00	103					
23		5	Saucer	Sunflower	6	1.50	3.00	69					

Outline button

Field with subtotals

7.10 Adding subtotals also outlines the list.

Note

When you've subtotaled list data and hidden part of it by collapsing the outline, it will print with that appearance. (The hidden data won't be printed.)

Understanding Excel's Table Feature

As if all the cool list functionality in Excel weren't enough, allow me to further satisfy your inner list maniac by introducing Excel's table capabilities. When you convert a regular range of data to a table, it becomes a named object with expanded capabilities to help with data management, analysis, and design. Read on to discover how you can upgrade from a plain old list to a table.

Converting a range to a table

You can create as many tables as needed on a single worksheet, because each table functions as an independent unit. That said, each range that you want to convert to a table should follow the same rules as when arranging a list. In particular, you want to make sure that there's a header row with labels for each column, and no blank rows or columns within the range. And, you want to make sure that blank columns and rows surround the table so that Excel can properly separate the table from any other data or tables on the sheet.

Genius

As part of prepping a range to convert to a table, you also should clear any cell styles that you've applied to cells in the range with Home → Editing → Clear → Clear Formats. (However, you may not want to clear formatting from cells with number formats applied.) Otherwise, the cell styles will fully or partially override the table style formatting, creating an inconsistent or perhaps even unreadable appearance in the affected cells.

Follow these steps to create a table with the default table style from the workbook theme:

1. **Click any cell in the range.**

2. **Choose Insert → Tables → Table or press Ctrl+T.** Excel selects the range to convert, which is why it's important to follow the layout rules. The Create Table dialog box also appears.

3. **Verify the settings in the Create Table dialog box.** You want to make sure that the whole table range is specified in the Where Is the Data for Your Table? text box and that the My Table Has Headers check box is checked.

4. **Click OK.** The conversion happens immediately, and the range is now a table.

5. **Click outside the table to deselect it.** You can now see the table formatting, as for the example shown in Figure 7.11.

Genius

There are two more ways to create a table with the default table style. Press Ctrl+Shift+* to select the list range, click the Quick Analysis button that appears at the lower-right corner, click Tables at the top of the pop-up that appears, and then click Table to instantly convert the range. The absolute fastest method is to click a cell in the table, press Ctrl+T, and just press Enter to accept the settings in the Create Table dialog box.

	A	B	C	D	E	F	G
1	Dinnerware Stock						
2							
3	ID	Item	Pattern	Size (in.)	Cost	Retail Price	# in Stock
4	1	Cup	Lily	3	2.50	5.00	73
5	2	Cereal Bowl	Rose	6	6.00	10.00	112
6	3	Saucer	Rose	6	1.50	3.00	88
7	4	Dinner Plate	Sunflower	10.5	10.00	20.00	51
8	5	Saucer	Sunflower	6	1.50	3.00	69
9	6	Soup Bowl	Lily	8	10.00	20.00	37
10	7	Salad Plate	Rose	8	4.25	8.50	115
11	8	Cup	Rose	3	2.50	5.00	144
12	9	Cereal Bowl	Lily	6	6.00	10.00	30
13	10	Saucer	Lily	6	1.50	3.00	133
14	11	Salad Plate	Sunflower	8	4.25	8.50	151
15	12	Soup Bowl	Sunflower	8	10.00	20.00	88
16	13	Soup Bowl	Rose	8	10.00	20.00	91
17	14	Cereal Bowl	Sunflower	6	6.00	10.00	58
18	15	Salad Plate	Lily	8	4.25	8.50	131
19	16	Dinner Plate	Rose	10.5	10.00	20.00	111
20	17	Cup	Sunflower	3	2.50	5.00	103
21	18	Dinner Plate	Lily	10.5	10.00	20.00	100
22							

7.11 Tables have their own styles and added features.

If you're interested in exploring the available table styles while converting a range to a table, the steps are slightly different:

1. **Click any cell in the range.**

2. **Choose Home → Styles → Format as Table.** The gallery of table styles appears. Move the mouse pointer over a style to see a descriptive ScreenTip. You may need to scroll down the gallery to view additional styles.

3. **Click the style to apply.** Excel selects the range to convert and opens the Format As Table dialog box.

4. **Verify the settings in the Format As Table dialog box.** You want to make sure that the whole table range is specified in the Where Is the Data for Your Table? text box and that the My Table Has Headers check box is checked.

5. **Click OK.** The conversion happens immediately, and the range is now a table.

6. **Click outside the table to deselect it.** The converted table has the style you selected in Step 3.

Note Ctrl+Shift+* selects the entire table after you've clicked a table cell. To select an entire column within the table, click a cell in the desired column, and press Ctrl+Spacebar. To select an entire row within the table, press Shift+Spacebar. The latter two shortcuts work outside of tables, too, and select the entire sheet column or row.

Importing or connecting to a list of data

If a list of data already exists in another type of file and you want to use that data in Excel, you can import the data into a new workbook file. Excel can readily import various types of files, so long as the data is properly structured. File types that Excel can import include delimited TXT and CSV files; various types of database files including Microsoft Access, HTML, and XML files; and more.

Choose File ➔ Open ➔ Browse, open the file type drop-down list, and choose the type of file to import. Then navigate to the location holding the file, click the file, and click Open. Some files, such as TXT and CSV files, open directly as a new workbook file. Then, all you need to do is choose File ➔ Save As.

For other file types, you may first see a Microsoft Excel Security Notice message, saying data connections have been blocked. Click Enable. Then, a dialog box like the Import Data dialog box shown in Figure 7.12 appears. In this case, when importing from an Access database file, the dialog box suggests importing the data as a table by default. Make your choices in the dialog box, and then click OK. If you see additional prompts or choices, respond to them as needed to import the data. Then save the file as needed.

Import Data	?	×
Select how you want to view this data in your workbook.		
⊙ Table		
○ PivotTable Report		
○ PivotChart		
○ Only Create Connection		
Where do you want to put the data?		
⊙ Existing worksheet:		
=$A$1		
○ New worksheet		
☐ Add this data to the Data Model		
Properties... ▾	OK	Cancel

7.12 Excel may prompt you for some details when you import data.

Figure 7.12 also includes an Only Create Connection option. What the heck does that mean, you ask? It means that the imported Access list, by default, has a *data connection* between the Excel workbook where you imported the data and the original Access file. Why would that be needed?

While Excel offers simple data functions, many organizations use full-blown relational databases or other comprehensive database management systems, some of which may be cloud-based. We're talking about thousands of rows (records) of data at a time, in many cases. This is not the sort of situation where it's easy to retype or even copy the data, for obvious reasons. Even worse, the data in your workbook would become out of date relative to the original source almost instantly, given the ongoing changes typically made to database information in large corporations.

The data connection enables Excel to retrieve updated data from the data source. It also enables you to query the data, if you have data query skills and want to give it a try. Sometimes the data connection itself is a query. The Get Data button in the Get & Transform Data group on the Data tab enables you to both import data and establish a connection to the data source. As shown in Figure 7.13, you can move the mouse pointer over any of the items in the Get Data menu to see the specific choices within that overall type of data source. (The menu's data source types can vary depending on the type of Microsoft 365 subscription you have and other factors, so your choices may differ from the ones in Figure 7.13.) The available choices both enable you to connect with data stored on a network and data stored using various cloud services and tools such as Azure and Salesforce.

After you choose a data source type, the process for connecting to it varies. You may be prompted to specify a URL for a data source, a server location, or a mailbox address, for example. Your organization's database administration pros can give you the information you need to connect with the data source. In the case of a file such as a database file on a network, the Import Data dialog box opens so that you can navigate to the file, click it, and click Import. Depending on the file type, from there you will see a window where you can preview the data or select which database object to import. Click Load to load the data as a table on a new sheet in the workbook. Click the main part of the Refresh All button any time you want to update the table with fresh data from the connected data source.

Genius

The Stocks and Geography buttons in the Data tab's Data Types group create updatable data. Type a stock ticker or place (such as a state) into a cell, reselect the cell, and click either Stocks or Geography. If prompted, make a choice in the Data Selector pane. To view data, click the stock or geography cell, click the Insert Data button that appears to the right, and choose the type of data to display. The requested statistic appears in the cell to the right.

Refresh All button

Get Data button

Data types

Data source types

7.13 Get Data both imports data as a table and creates a data connection.

Changing table styles

If the default table style or a style you selected when creating the table no longer suits your needs, it's easy to change it. When you click a cell in the table, the Table Design tab becomes available. Click the Table Design tab, and then click the Quick Styles button in the Table Styles group to open the gallery of styles. Use the mouse to Live Preview a new design on your table (see Figure 7.14), and then click the winning style to apply it.

Table Design tab

Table Name box

Table Style Options

| File | Home | Insert | Page Layout | Formulas | Data | Review | View | Help | Table Design | | ⊘ Share | ⊡ Comments | ☺ |

Table Name:
Table6

- Summarize with PivotTable
- Remove Duplicates
- ⊕ Resize Table
- Convert to Range

Properties | Tools

Insert Slicer

Export Refresh

External Table Data

- ☑ Header Row
- ☐ Total Row
- ☑ Banded Rows
- ☐ First Column
- ☐ Last Column
- ☐ Banded Columns
- ☑ Filter Button

Quick Styles

Light

White, Table Style Light 1

Medium

F8 | × ✓ fx | 3

	A	B	C	D	E	F	G
1	Dinnerware Stock						
2							
3	ID	Item	Pattern	Size (in.)	Cost	Retail Price	# in Stock
4	1	Cup	Lily	3	2.50	5.00	
5	2	Cereal Bowl	Rose	6	6.00	10.00	
6	3	Saucer	Rose	6	1.50	3.00	
7	4	Dinner Plate	Sunflower	10.5	10.00	20.00	
8	5	Saucer	Sunflower	6	1.50	3.00	
9	6	Soup Bowl	Lily	8	10.00	20.00	
10	7	Salad Plate	Rose	8	4.25	8.50	
11	8	Cup	Rose	3	2.50	5.00	
12	9	Cereal Bowl	Lily	6	6.00	10.00	
13	10	Saucer	Lily	6	1.50	3.00	
14	11	Salad Plate	Sunflower	8	4.25	8.50	
15	12	Soup Bowl	Sunflower	8	10.00	20.00	
16	13	Soup Bowl	Rose	8	10.00	20.00	
17	14	Cereal Bowl	Sunflower	6	6.00	10.00	
18	15	Salad Plate	Lily	8	4.25	8.50	
19	16	Dinner Plate	Rose	10.5	10.00	20.00	
20	17	Cup	Sunflower	3	2.50	5.00	
21	18	Dinner Plate	Lily	10.5	10.00	20.00	
22							
23							
24							

New Table Style...

Clear

7.14 A new table style quickly updates a table's appearance.

To the left of the Table Styles group of the Table Design tab, several choices for controlling specific aspects of the table style appear in the Table Style Options group. Click to check or uncheck those check boxes to choose whether to display special formatting for items such as banded rows or banded columns.

Resizing a table

When you add new information in a row below a table or a column to the right of a table, the table automatically expands to encompass the new information. Excel automatically applies the appropriate table style to the additional information. This convenient feature means you don't have to spend your time manually applying formatting.

You also can resize a table before entering new data in it. The bottom-right corner of the bottom-right cell in a table has a little blue triangle that is the sizing handle for the table. You can drag it to increase or decrease the number of columns or rows in the table. This sizing handle doesn't let you drag diagonally.

Renaming a table

Excel assigns a generic name to each table you add to the workbook file, as in *Table1*, *Table2*, and so on. You can rename the table by clicking a table cell, selecting the contents of the Table Design → Properties → Table Name text box (refer to Figure 7.14), typing a new name, and pressing Enter. The same general rules for what a range name can include apply to table names. For a refresher about those, jump back to "Creating Range Names" in Chapter 2.

Why bother changing the table name? Two reasons come to mind immediately. If you have multiple tables on the current sheet, you can use the Name box to select a particular table. Having more descriptive table names applied will make that navigation trick easier. Plus, table names on the current sheet appear in the Go To dialog box that appears when you press Ctrl+G or F5, and the more explanatory table names will make it clearer where you want to go.

Sorting and Filtering a Table

Being honest here: sorting and filtering a table isn't really different than sorting a list of data, as described earlier in this chapter, in the "Sorting, Filtering, and Subtotaling Lists of Information" section. You can revisit that section to go over the details of using the Sort & Filter group choices on the Data tab again.

The most important distinction to know is that by default a filter button appears on each header row cell in a table so that you don't have to display them manually. Clicking a filter button displays the same choices for sorting and filtering as when you turn on filtering for a regular list, as shown in Figure 7.15.

> **Genius**
>
> The Table Design → Table Style Options → Filter Button check box enables you to toggle the table header filter buttons on and off, as does the Data → Sort & Filter → Filter button. You might want to turn them off to discourage other users from filtering the table, for example.

Using Table Calculations

You can add calculations to a table just like any other range of data. Tables have some bonus functionality when it comes to making calculations, and this part of the chapter explains how those bonuses pay off.

▲	A	B	C	D	E
1	Dinnerware Stock				
2					
3	ID ▾	Item ▾	Pattern ▾	Size (in.) ▾	Cost ▾

A↓ Sort A to Z	3 · 2.50
Z↓ Sort Z to A	6 · 6.00
	6 · 1.50
Sort by Color >	10.5 · 10.00
Sheet View >	6 · 1.50
	8 · 10.00
▽ Clear Filter From "Pattern"	8 · 4.25
Filter by Color >	3 · 2.50
Text Filters >	6 · 6.00
	6 · 1.50
Search 🔍	8 · 4.25
☑ (Select All)	8 · 10.00
☑ Lily	8 · 10.00
☑ Rose	6 · 6.00
☑ Sunflower	8 · 4.25
	10.5 · 10.00
	3 · 2.50
	10.5 · 10.00
OK Cancel	:inerware Stock (2)

7.15 Filter buttons appear by default on the table header row.

Adding a calculated column

In many cases, you will add a new calculation in the column immediately to the right of the table. This is also called adding a *calculated column* to the table. The formulas in a table's calculated column use a special kind of references called *structured references*. The structured references usually include the table and column name, as in TableName[ColumnName], but in some cases the table name can be omitted when the formula refers to columns in the current table. Often, @ needs to be included with the column name, as in [@ColumnName], to be sure to refer to the current row only in the formula. By showing the column name in particular in the formula, a structured reference more clearly identifies exactly what input information the formula uses for its calculations.

Note

Structured references can get pretty complicated from this simple explanation. To learn more, I suggest searching Help or Microsoft's online support offerings for the article titled "Using structured references with Excel tables."

171

Follow these steps to add a calculated column to a table:

1. **Type a column name in the header cell in the column immediately to the right of the header row and press Enter.** When you press Enter, the rest of the cells in the column take on the style of the rest of the table.

2. **In the second cell of the new column, type = (equals), and then create the formula, using the mouse to select cells or ranges. Or you can type in the structured references as indicated earlier.** As shown in Figure 7.16, when you type the formula with structured references, the Formula AutoComplete feature kicks in after you type the table name and first square bracket, showing you the available columns. Highlight a choice and press Tab or just double-click it to enter it into the formula. Excel uses color coding in the table and the formula to identify and match up referenced columns.

Formula AutoComplete lists table columns
Structured reference

A	B	C	D	E	F	G	H	I
Dinnerware Stock								
ID	Item	Pattern	Size (in.)	Cost	Retail Price	# in Stock	Inventory Cost	
1	Cup	Lily	3	2.50	5.00	73	=DS[@Cost]*DS[@[	
2	Cereal Bowl	Rose	6	6.00	10.00	112		
3	Saucer	Rose	6	1.50	3.00	88		
4	Dinner Plate	Sunflower	10.5	10.00	20.00	51		
5	Saucer	Sunflower	6	1.50	3.00	69		
6	Soup Bowl	Lily	8	10.00	20.00	37		
7	Salad Plate	Rose	8	4.25	8.50	115		
8	Cup	Rose	3	2.50	5.00	144		
9	Cereal Bowl	Lily	6	6.00	10.00	30		
10	Saucer	Lily	6	1.50	3.00	133		
11	Salad Plate	Sunflower	8	4.25	8.50	151		
12	Soup Bowl	Sunflower	8	10.00	20.00	88		
13	Soup Bowl	Rose	8	10.00	20.00	91		
14	Cereal Bowl	Sunflower	6	6.00	10.00	58		
15	Salad Plate	Lily	8	4.25	8.50	131		
16	Dinner Plate	Rose	10.5	10.00	20.00	111		
17	Cup	Sunflower	3	2.50	5.00	103		
18	Dinner Plate	Lily	10.5	10.00	20.00	100		

AutoComplete dropdown:
(...) ID
(...) Item
(...) Pattern
(...) Size (in.)
(...) Cost
(...) Retail Price
(...) # in Stock
(...) Inventory Cost

7.16 Table calculated columns use structured references.

Caution It can be tough to get the formula syntax right with structured references, so I prefer using the mouse to create the formula for a table calculated column. That said, if you try to do it by typing and get a message with a suggested correction, study the correction carefully for learning purposes.

3. **Finish the formula by typing any closing brackets or parentheses, and then press Enter.** The formula fills or expands down the calculated column automatically. Note that you might want or need to change the number formatting for the column, such as adjusting the number of decimal places.

Adding a total row

Displaying a total row below a table falls right into that bucket labeled "Work Smarter, not Harder." The total row enables you to select a function to perform a calculation on the data in the column above. It takes only a few steps:

1. **Click a cell in the table.**

2. **Choose Table Design → Table Style Options → Total Row.** You are clicking the Total Row check box to check it in this case. To hide the total row later, you would clear the check box.

3. **Click the total row cell below the column to calculate, click the arrow button, and then click the function to apply.** As shown in Figure 7.17, several of the usual suspect functions appear on the list, or you can choose More Functions to select another function.

	A	B	C	D	E	F	G	H
1	Dinnerware Stock							
2								
3	ID	Item	Pattern	Size (in.)	Cost	Retail Price	# in Stock	Inventory Cost
4	1	Cup	Lily	3	2.50	5.00	73	182.50
5	2	Cereal Bowl	Rose	6	6.00	10.00	112	672.00
6	3	Saucer	Rose	6	1.50	3.00	88	132.00
7	4	Dinner Plate	Sunflower	10.5	10.00	20.00	51	510.00
8	5	Saucer	Sunflower	6	1.50	3.00	69	103.50
9	6	Soup Bowl	Lily	8	10.00	20.00	37	370.00
10	7	Salad Plate	Rose	8	4.25	8.50	115	488.75
11	8	Cup	Rose	3	2.50	5.00	144	360.00
12	9	Cereal Bowl	Lily	6	6.00	10.00	30	180.00
13	10	Saucer	Lily	6	1.50	3.00	133	199.50
14	11	Salad Plate	Sunflower	8	4.25	8.50	151	641.75
15	12	Soup Bowl	Sunflower	8	None	20.00	88	880.00
16	13	Soup Bowl	Rose	8	Average	20.00	91	910.00
17	14	Cereal Bowl	Sunflower	6	Count / Count Number	10.00	58	348.00
18	15	Salad Plate	Lily	8	Max	8.50	131	556.75
19	16	Dinner Plate	Rose	10.5	Min / Sum	20.00	111	1110.00
20	17	Cup	Sunflower	3	StdDev	5.00	103	257.50
21	18	Dinner Plate	Lily	10.5	Var / More Function	20.00	100	1000.00
22	Total							8902.25
23								

7.17 Choose the function to use to calculate a column in a total row cell.

173

4. **Repeat Step 3 to choose functions in other total row cells as desired.** Excel automatically inserts the SUM function for the far right column, so you should change or remove that function (None is one of the function choices) as dictated by your data.

Converting a Table Back to a Range of Regular Cells

Converting a table back to a range will be the one of the easiest things we've done in the chapter, so it will be a nice way to wrap up our discussion of tables. One cool thing about the result is that the range retains the formatting from the table style. It looks just as attractive as the table, but it lacks the table functionality, which is the point of the conversion. You may want or need to convert a table back to a regular range if the table functionality creates a problem with copying the table's contents to another application. To convert a table back to a range of regular cells, follow these steps:

1. **Click a cell in the table.**

2. **Choose Table Design → Tools → Convert to Range.**

3. **Click Yes when prompted to confirm the conversion.**

How Do I Present My Data in Charts?

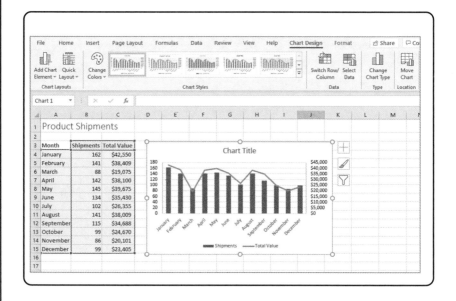

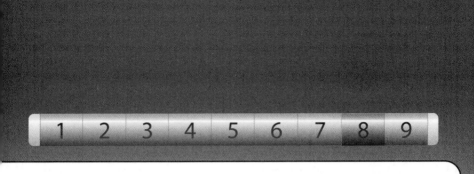

You've probably heard the buzzy term *data visualization* thrown around a lot lately. Excel charts are one form of data visualization, along with maps and other diagrams. Excel enables you to create numerous types of charts to present data in accessible visual formats. Because Excel's charting tools are so flexible, you can deploy charts in a variety of ways in a workbook and apply different layouts and formatting. This chapter mentors you in data visualization skills, including creating, formatting, changing, moving, and deleting Excel charts, with a final look at some special types of charts.

Charts and Their Role in Your Workbooks

An Excel chart presents a graphical or visual representation of a selected set of data. In Chapter 6, I compared the graphics you can work with in Excel to elements of many infographics, which present a narrative through text, data, graphics, and charts. A chart you create in Excel can be used as part of an infographic approach or can stand alone as a data visualization.

Charts don't just make a worksheet prettier. They visually summarize and simplify the data. Some people are visual learners and can absorb and comprehend data more quickly when the data is presented in chart form. In this context, including a chart in addition to the numeric information can help more readers understand the significance of the data you're reporting. This makes a chart an outstanding aid for organizational decision-making. Just to name a few examples, charts can help to do the following:

- **Show how discrete values compare.** Pinpoint the best and worst data points.

- **Present how parts of a whole or level compare.** Identify the biggest contributing items in a total.

- **Illustrate trends and performance over time.** More clearly reveal improvements or declines.

- **Emphasize magnitude of change.** Large differences become more apparent when charted.

- **Find data outliers.** When a stat such as a test result is really outside of the norm for the rest of the data, a chart can reveal it.

- **Depict other types of statistical information.** Explore how multiple sets of data compare and show positive and negative changes, data distribution, and more.

You're not limited to just data, chart, data, chart on a worksheet. You can use the Excel charts in other ways, such as the following:

- **Copy and paste a chart into other types of documents.** For example, if you're writing a report in Word about the data you've gathered and evaluated, you could paste a chart of that data. In Word, the pasted chart would be linked to the original Excel source file by default. This is important because Excel charts update automatically when the underlying data changes. You also could use Paste Special to paste the copied chart as a static graphic in the destination document.

● **Save a chart as a file.** You can paste a copied chart into a graphics program such as Windows Paint, crop out any excess whitespace around it, and then save the image in the desired graphic or picture file format. This technique can be handy when you want to insert the chart in multiple documents, when you definitely need for the chart to be a static image, or when you want to include the chart graphic in an email message or web page.

● **Build a dashboard to summarize key data updates.** If a workbook file has a lot of key data or metrics that you frequently update, you can create a dashboard sheet. The dashboard would typically be the first sheet in the workbook, with multiple charts charting the data from the other sheet. Use Cut (Ctrl+X) and Paste (Ctrl+V) to move each chart from the source data sheet where you created it to the dashboard sheet. Remember, the charts will update automatically whenever the data changes, so the dashboard gives an at-a-glance overview as the data changes. Even better, if you connected lists of data from outside databases and other sources as explained in Chapter 7, any updates made to the outside sources flow right to your sheets and the related dashboard charts. Talk about business intelligence.

Chart Types

Excel includes dozens of chart types you can use to illustrate data. That said, you need to use the right chart type for your data; otherwise, your chart will provide visual *mis*information. Table 8.1 provides a general overview of the overall chart types. Each category includes multiple subtypes, or the specific variants of the main chart type that you can apply when you create a chart. For example, some chart types have 2-D and 3-D subtypes. Table 8.1 also mentions a subtype or two within each category.

Table 8.1 Overall Chart Types in Excel

Name	Description and Subtype Examples
Column or Bar	Compares discrete values from a few categories. Subtypes include Clustered Column and 3-D Stacked Bar.
Line or Area	Compares many points of data to illustrate trends, usually over time. Subtypes include Line with Markers and 3-D Area.
Pie or Doughnut	Identifies proportions of a whole, with the whole assumed to be 100%. Choose a Pie subtype to chart a single series, and choose Doughnut for multiple series. Subtypes include Pie of Pie and 3-D Pie.

continued

Table 8.1 continued

Name	Description and Subtype Examples
Hierarchy	Identifies proportions of a whole, when the data is organized in a hierarchy of categories. Subtypes include Treemap and Sunburst.
Statistic	Evaluates and presents the data in common statistical analysis charts. Subtypes include Pareto and Box and Whisker.
Scatter (X,Y) or Bubble	Illustrates the relationship between multiple sets of values. Subtypes include Scatter with Smooth Lines and Markers and Scatter with Straight Lines.
Waterfall, Funnel, Stock, Surface or Radar	Catchall category with special-purpose charts listed in the category name. Subtypes include Wireframe 3-D Surface and Radar with Markers.
Combo	Compares mixed values or values that vary greatly in scale along two axes using two chart types. Subtypes include Clustered Column - Line on Secondary Axis and Stacked Area - Clustered Column.

The Charts group of the Insert tab, shown in Figure 8.1, has a button for each general chart type listed in Table 8.1. As for other galleries or lists of choices shown earlier in the book, you can click a chart type button and then move the mouse pointer over one of the choices to see a descriptive ScreenTip and a preview of how the chart would look if applied to the selected data. Often you'll be able to see right away if a particular chart depicts the data in a misleading or nonmeaningful way.

Creating a Chart

The first step in creating any chart is to select the data to be charted. But you can't just select any old data. Excel must be able to identify each *series* and *category* of data in the selected range. Usually, each series is contained in a single row or single column, with each item in the series being called a single *data point* that's charted with a column, pie wedge, or other data marker, depending on the chart type. Categories group similar data points in some chart types.

 Caution You generally do not want to select any total row or column when creating a chart, because that would skew the appearance of the charted data. The possible exception is for pie charts, when you might *only* select the total data.

8.1 Use the Chart type buttons in the Charts group of the Insert tab to explore the available charts.

For Figure 8.1, I selected the range A3:C15. Excel correctly identified that the Shipments entries in column B formed one series, and the Total Value entries in column C formed a second series. And yes, it's a good idea to include row and column labels in the selection so that Excel can use them to label parts of the chart. Because the series varied widely in scale, the combo chart being previewed looked good. I could have just clicked to apply that subtype to the chart. Note that other chart types, such as High-Low-Close, require for the data series to be arranged in a more particular order.

> **Caution**
>
> If you select multiple series and create a pie chart, Excel charts only the first series of data, because pie charts show only one series. Each data point in the series becomes a slice in the pie. What if the labels for your data points are one or more rows or columns away from the series itself, such as having the labels in column A and the series in column D? Select the labels, Ctrl+drag to select the series, and then create the pie chart.

Selecting the data to chart and then using the Insert → Charts choices to create a chart is one way to create a chart, but there are numerous others. Excel now has built-in intelligence to analyze the chart data and recommend appropriate chart types, a feature called *Recommended Charts*. You can choose your own chart type or a recommended one in these additional ways to create a chart after you've selected the data to chart:

- **Insert Chart dialog box.** Click the Charts group dialog box launcher on the Insert tab to open this dialog box. On the Recommended Charts tab (see Figure 8.2), you can click a thumbnail from the suggestions at the left to see a larger preview and description and then click OK to choose that chart type. Alternately, you can click the All Charts tab and click choices at the left and the top to preview various chart types; then click OK to create the desired chart.

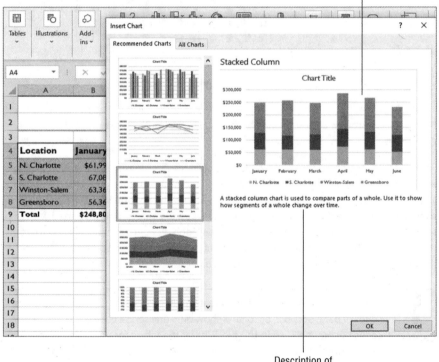

8.2 The Insert Chart dialog box offers Recommended Charts.

- **Quick Analysis.** After you select the range to chart, click the Quick Analysis button that appears at the lower-right corner or press Ctrl+Q. Click Charts at the top of the pop-up, move the mouse pointer over a button for a Recommended Charts suggestion to see a preview, and then click the chart type to create.

- **Ideas Pane.** Choose Home → Ideas → Ideas to open the Ideas pane, which analyzes the data, displays suggested charts, and enables you to ask questions about the data. As shown in the example in Figure 8.3, you can scroll down to see additional results and options. Click Insert Chart within a chart thumbnail to create a chart as shown in the preview, and then close the pane.

Click to create chart
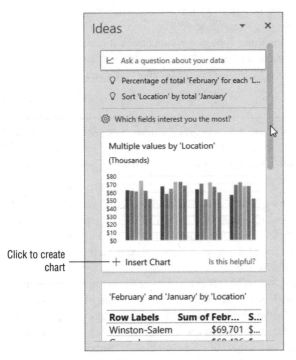

8.3 The Ideas pane enables you to ask questions about the data and create a chart.

Genius

If you're incorporating numerous charts in a workbook file or on a dashboard sheet, sticking with similar chart types will make the design much more cohesive. For example, you probably don't want to mix 2-D and 3-D chart types. Some designers prefer not to use 3-D charts at all, arguing that they can distort the relative appearance of the data, especially for 3-D pie charts.

The final step to creating a chart is moving it into the position you want and resizing it if needed. As for other graphics that you learned about in Chapter 6, you can click a chart to select it. Then you can drag it into the desired position on the sheet or press and hold the Shift key while dragging a corner handle to resize the chart proportionally. You also can cut, copy, and paste the selected chart. Click outside the chart to deselect it.

Changing the Chart Type and Layout

After you create a chart, elements of the chart, including the chart type, aren't set in stone. When you select a chart, the Chart Design and Format contextual tabs appear with settings for changing or refining the chart's appearance. If you choose Chart Design → Type → Change Chart Type, the Change Chart Type dialog box opens. It looks and works just like the Insert Chart dialog box shown in Figure 8.2. You can use the choices on either the Recommended Charts or All Charts tab to select another chart type and then click OK to apply the change.

Note

> You also can use the Insert → Charts group choices to preview and change the chart type for the selected chart.

Beyond changing the overall chart type, a chart has many different elements that you can edit or reformat, as shown in Figure 8.4. Obviously, you would want to change the Chart Title placeholder contents to a more descriptive title, and the next section covers making those kinds of changes. The plot area is where the data is plotted, usually along two axes for most chart types: the horizontal (category) axis and the vertical (value) axis. In the example in Figure 8.4, you can see that the months appear as the categories along the horizontal (category) axis, and the values for the first series, Shipments, appear beside the vertical (value) axis at left. The Shipments series is plotted as a column chart. (If multiple series of monthly data had been plotted as the column chart, each month category would include a column for each series.) Because the example is a combination chart with a line chart used to show the values for the Total Value series, a secondary vertical (value) axis appears to the right of the plot area to show the values for the line chart. A legend at the bottom of the chart shows the name, color, and shape or appearance for each series of data in the chart.

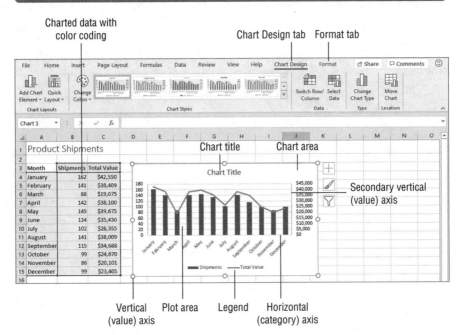

8.4 The position of chart elements depends on the layout applied.

Note

The horizontal (category) axis used to be called the *x-axis*, and the vertical (value) axis used to be called the *y-axis*, as in traditional mathematics.

If you want to change the overall arrangements of the elements in the chart, you can do so quickly by changing the layout. The layout controls which chart elements appear and where they appear and in some cases modifies the sizing or spacing for elements such as column chart data points (columns). To preview and change the layout for the selected chart, choose Chart Design → Chart Layouts → Quick Layout. Move the mouse pointer over a layout in the gallery to view a Live Preview on the chart and see a ScreenTip listing the elements included in the layout. Figure 8.5 shows the same chart as Figure 8.4 with a preview of a different layout. The previewed layout doesn't include a chart title, adds horizontal (category) and vertical (value) axis titles, changes the angle of the category labels, moves the legend from below the chart to the right of the chart, and uses a different background for the plot area. To apply one of the layouts, click it in the gallery.

Change Chart Type button

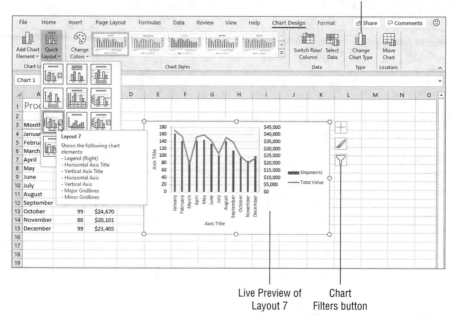

Live Preview of Layout 7   Chart Filters button

8.5 Use the Quick Layout gallery to preview and apply a new layout.

Genius

Too many data points can overload some chart types. Some data visualization experts recommend that a pie chart have no more than five or six data point slices. In a line chart with markers, the data points can become indistinguishable and nonmeaningful when crammed together on a small chart. To fix the situation, examine your data and consider whether you can group or categorize it, or perhaps use the Chart Filters button (see Figure 8.5) to limit the displayed data.

Formatting Chart Elements

You can edit and format chart elements individually as needed to meet your design and communications objectives. For example, you would obviously want to replace the placeholder text for the chart title or an axis title. To do so, select the chart, and then click the title or axis element on the chart area so that a selection box with blue handles appears around it. Type the text to add, which appears in the Formula bar as you type, and then click outside the element selection box. While a box for a text element is selected, you also can use the choices in the Font group of the Home tab and the Shape Styles and WordArt Styles groups of the Format tab. These formatting choices work as described earlier in the book, especially in Chapter 6.

Genius

To use text contained in a cell as the chart title or an axis title, select the title box on the chart, click in the Formula Bar, type the = (equals) sign, click the cell that holds the title text, and then press Enter. If you later update the cell contents, the title updates automatically in the chart.

As for other graphics in Excel, the default formatting for charts comes via the theme applied to the workbook file. The Chart Styles group of the Chart Design tab offers two galleries: one for changing just the colors for the chart (Change Colors) and another for changing the chart style (Chart Styles). The chart style controls fonts; fill for the data markers, plot area, and chart area; and even effects such as shadows and gradients. Just open either gallery, move the mouse pointer over a choice to see a Live Preview (see Figure 8.6), and then click the color combo or style to apply.

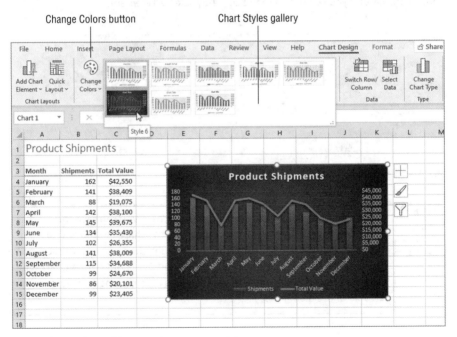

8.6 Update a chart with new colors or a new style.

If you don't need to change the overall layout for the chart but want to add or remove a particular chart element, use the Chart Design ➔ Chart Layouts ➔ Add Chart Element menu. For example, you could choose Chart Design ➔ Chart Layouts ➔ Add Chart Element ➔ Chart Title ➔ None to remove the chart title. Or you could choose Chart Design ➔ Chart Layouts ➔ Add Chart Element ➔ Axis Titles ➔ Primary Vertical to add a placeholder for a vertical (value) axis title, to which you could add the desired text. This menu offers many choices for adding, removing, and repositioning chart elements. For example, you can move the legend to the right side of the chart. Or, you can add a data table to include the data being charted within the chart area, which is handy if you want to include the chart in another document or save it as a graphic image file.

Some elements of a chart, such as an axis, are tricky to select for formatting. The Chart Elements drop-down list at the top of the Current Selection group at the left end of the Format tab (see Figure 8.7) enables you to select a specific chart element prior to formatting it or otherwise making changes. Choose the item to select in the list, and then use the tools on the Format tab as needed to update the selected element's appearance. You could also choose Format ➔ Current Selection ➔ Format Selection to open a Format pane with detailed formatting choices or Format ➔ Current Selection ➔ Reset to Match Style to remove formatting you've applied to the currently selected element.

File	Home	Insert	Page Layout	Formulas	Data	Review	View	Help	Chart Design	Format	Share	Comments	

Chart Area
- Chart Area
- Chart Title
- Horizontal (Category) Axis
- Legend
- Plot Area
- Secondary Vertical (Value) Axis
- Vertical (Value) Axis
- Vertical (Value) Axis Major Gridlines
- Series "Shipments"
- Series "Total Value"

Product Shipments

8.7 Select a chart element to format.

Genius

If you've invested a lot of time customizing a chart, you can save the chart as a template that you can use again. Right-click the chart, choose Save as Template, edit the filename, and click Save. (Do not change the save location.) You can find and use the template in the Insert Chart or Change Chart Type dialog boxes by clicking the All Charts tab and then clicking Templates at the left side of the dialog box.

Some users like to get fancy and add a bold color fill or even a texture or picture fill to the chart area, which is essentially the background for the entire chart. If you go with a treatment like that, be judicious. (Or to put it another way, don't get too crazy.) Make sure that all of the other chart elements remain clear and readable in context with the chosen background.

Changing the Charted Data

A callout in Figure 8.4 showed how when a chart is selected, Excel highlights the charted data with color coding and selection outlines, similar to the color coding used for cell and range references when you are creating or editing a formula. The cells holding the charted data appear in blue, while red is used for series labels and purple is used for category labels. And, as for a formula, any time you change a label or value in a charted range, the chart updates to reflect your changes. This dynamic relationship between the underlying data and the chart ensures that they remain in sync.

That doesn't mean that you can't adjust the relationship, however. For example, if each series or category of the data is held in a column, but Excel assumed each was held in a row, you can flip the relationship by selecting the chart and then choosing Chart Design → Data → Switch Row/Column. The left stacked column chart shown in Figure 8.8 is an example where Excel assumed that each series was held in a row. I applied Switch Row/Column to the copy of the chart on the right to indicate that the series are held in columns.

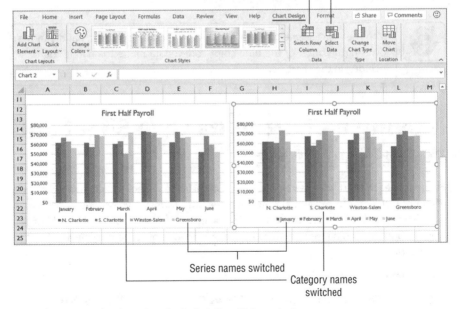

8.8 Adjust series plotting using the Switch Row/Column button.

In other cases, you may need to change the range of data that's charted. Choose Chart Design → Data → Select Data to open the Select Data Source dialog box shown in Figure 8.9. Either edit the entry in the Chart Data Range text box or use the collapse button at the far end of the text box to collapse the dialog box so that you select the range with the mouse and then re-expand the dialog box. Click OK, and the chart adjusts to show the data from the newly selected range.

Charted range

▲	A	B	C	D	E	F	G	H	I	J	K
4	Location	January	February	March	April	May	June	Total	Average		
5	N. Charlotte	$61,994	$61,689								
6	S. Charlotte	67,080	57,602								
7	Winston-Salem	63,364	69,701								
8	Greensboro	56,366	68,436								
9	Total	$248,804	$257,428								

Select Data Source dialog:

Chart data range: =Sheet6!$A$4:$G$8

Switch Row/Column

Legend Entries (Series):
- Add, Edit, × Remove
- ☑ January
- ☑ February
- ☑ March
- ☑ April
- ☑ May

Horizontal (Category) Axis Labels:
- Edit
- ☑ N. Charlotte
- ☑ S. Charlotte
- ☑ Winston-Salem
- ☑ Greensboro

Hidden and Empty Cells   OK   Cancel

8.9 You can change the source data range for the selected chart.

Genius

With the chart selected, you also can drag the blue selection handle in the lower-right corner of the blue color-coded data range to change the data included in the chart.

Moving a Chart to Its Own Sheet and Deleting a Chart

By default, each chart you create is an object on the sheet where you created it. Because it's an object, you can move it around the sheet and format it as previously discussed. You also can move the chart to its own sheet, called a *chart sheet*. You might do this if you want to print a clean handout with just the chart. Follow these steps to move a chart to a chart sheet:

1. **Select the chart by clicking it.**

2. **Choose Chart Design → Location → Move Chart, or right-click the chart and choose Move Chart.** The Move Chart dialog box appears.

3. **Click the New Sheet option button.** As shown in Figure 8.10, you can optionally edit the name in the accompanying text box.

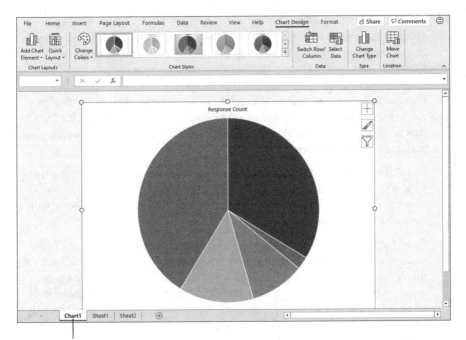

8.10 Move the chart to a separate chart sheet.

4. **Click OK.** Excel creates a new sheet for the chart and moves it there. As shown in Figure 8.11, when you select the chart on the chart sheet, the Chart Design and Format tabs appear on the ribbon as usual so that you can make changes to the chart as desired.

Chart sheet

8.11 Select the chart on the chart sheet to display the Chart Design and Format tabs.

191

Note

You can select a range of data to chart and then press F11 to create a new chart on its own chart sheet. From there, you can change the chart type and formatting as needed.

You can delete a chart from any sheet. Just click the chart, and press the Delete key on the keyboard. Without warning, there goes the chart to the great chart dustbin. If you need the chart back, press Ctrl+Z or click the Undo button on the QAT right away. You can't delete a chart from a chart sheet, but you can delete the chart sheet. Right-click the Sheet tab and choose Delete. In the message box that warns that the chart will be permanently deleted, click Delete.

Using Special Charts: Sparklines, PivotTables, and Maps

To close out the chapter, I want to present a few examples of other chart possibilities. Have fun later when you experiment with these special chart types:

- **Sparklines.** These are little one-cell mini charts that you usually place to the right of a row of values. Click the blank cell to the right of a row, choose Insert ➔ Sparklines, and then choose one of the three sparkline types. In the Create Sparklines dialog box, specify the Data Range, and then click OK. You can then fill the sparkline down the column. Figure 8.12 shows some sparklines charting the values from columns B:G and skipping the totals and averages. (For me, the Data Bar conditional formatting from the Home ➔ Conditional Formatting menu shown in Figure 5.17 also produces clear one-cell mini charts.)

- **PivotTables and PivotCharts.** These are for summarizing and charting complex data, with the power to rearrange and reanalyze the data. If you choose File ➔ New and then scroll down, you can click the Make Your First PivotTable (PivotTable Tutorial) thumbnail for a tutorial on getting started.

- **Filled Map.** If you've tried applying the Geography data type (Data ➔ Data Types ➔ Geography) and then displaying some numeric data as touched on in Chapter 7, then you may be able to create a filled map chart that represents the data geographically. Click any cell in the data range, and then choose Insert ➔ Charts ➔ Maps ➔ Filled Map. If it can, Excel connects with the Internet and creates the map. Figure 8.13 shows an example. Fair warning, though: this feature is finicky and can recognize only certain types of data.

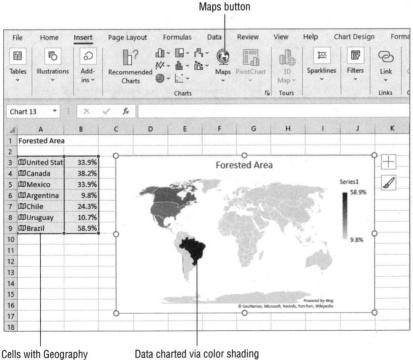

Sparklines button

First Half Payroll

2Day Tech Services, LLC

Location	January	February	March	April	May	June	Total	Average
N. Charlotte	$61,994	$61,689	$60,654	$73,690	$61,721	$51,680	$371,428	$61,905
S. Charlotte	67,080	57,602	63,437	72,441	72,458	68,037	$401,055	$66,843
Winston-Salem	63,364	69,701	50,541	71,780	66,321	59,296	$381,003	$63,501
Greensboro	56,366	68,436	71,936	66,947	67,247	51,614	$382,546	$63,758
Total	**$248,804**	**$257,428**	**$246,568**	**$284,858**	**$267,747**	**$230,627**	**$1,536,032**	**$256,005**

Sparklines

8.12 Sparklines are one-cell mini charts.

Maps button

Forested Area

United Stat	33.9%
Canada	38.2%
Mexico	33.9%
Argentina	9.8%
Chile	24.3%
Uruguay	10.7%
Brazil	58.9%

Forested Area

Series1
58.9%

9.8%

Powered by Bing
© GeoNames, Microsoft, Navinfo, TomTom, Wikipedia

Cells with Geography
data type

Data charted via color shading

8.13 Excel grabs data from the Internet to create a filled map.

How Do I Print and Share My Content?

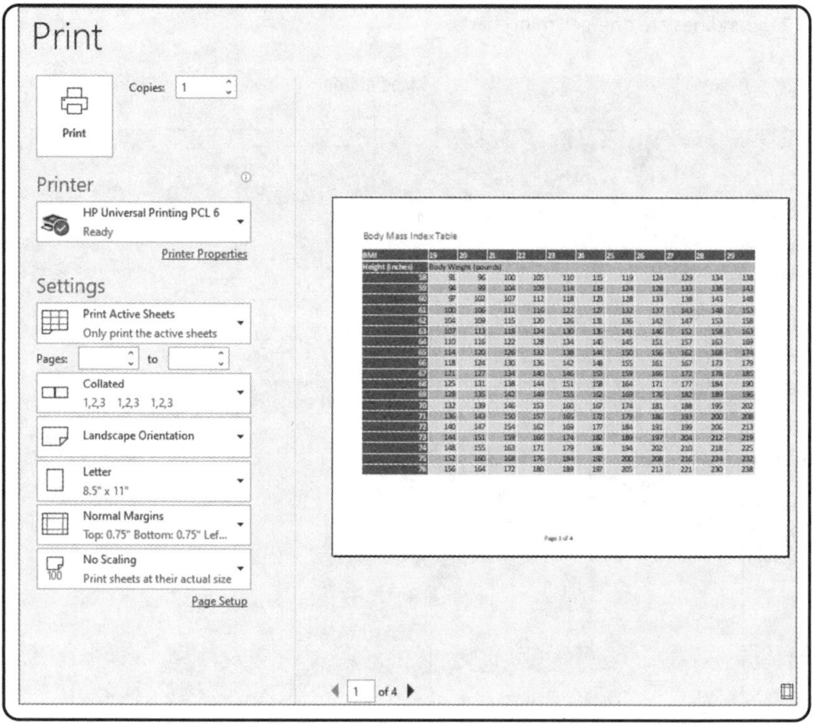

Print

Copies: 1

Print

Printer

HP Universal Printing PCL 6
Ready

Printer Properties

Settings

Print Active Sheets
Only print the active sheets

Pages: ___ to ___

Collated
1,2,3   1,2,3   1,2,3

Landscape Orientation

Letter
8.5" x 11"

Normal Margins
Top: 0.75" Bottom: 0.75" Lef...

No Scaling
Print sheets at their actual size

Page Setup

Body Mass Index Table

1 of 4

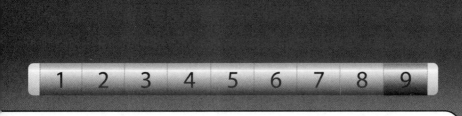

As organizations increasingly digitize document workflows to cut costs, some situations still justify the convenience or relative permanence of a paper printout. A project estimate you've created in Excel might require the client's signature. You might want to print a to-do list for portability. A colleague might want a hard copy of your sheets. Each Excel worksheet's large size can cause unruly printouts. This chapter covers Printout Wrangling 101, from creating headers and footers, to controlling page and sheet appearance, to handling page breaks, through previewing and printing. I throw in a couple of nonprinting sharing methods as a bonus.

Creating Headers and Footers

To add further identifying information to a printout, you can add a header or footer. A header prints in the margin at the top of each page, while a footer prints in the margin at the bottom of each page. While a one-page printout might not need headers and footers as much, it's definitely a professional touch to include a header or footer with page numbering for any multipage printout.

The first step for setting up a header or footer is to choose Insert ➔ Text ➔ Header & Footer. This automatically changes to Page Layout view and places the insertion point in the center box of the header. The Page Layout view shows the page margins and breaks and includes horizontal and vertical rulers.

Alternately, you could choose View ➔ Workbook Views ➔ Page Layout and then click the grayed-out Add Header or Add Footer text in a margin area to display the header and footer areas. (You have to scroll down to see the footer area at the bottom of the page.) The header and footer both have left, right, and center boxes that you can click in and then type entries or choose a type of content to add.

Next, you use the tools on the Header & Footer tab (see Figure 9.1) that appears to create the header and/or footer contents, and there are a lot of choices and possible combinations. If you click either the Header or Footer button in the Header & Footer group, a menu of available presets appears. Presets insert such information as the page number, the sheet name, *Confidential* plus the date and page number, and so on.

To insert elements manually, first click in the desired box in the header or footer. (Use the buttons in the Header & Footer ➔ Navigation group to jump between the header and footer.) You can type some descriptive text, if desired. Or, click the desired button in the Header & Footer Elements group to insert the desired element. In some cases, such as if you click Page Number, Excel immediately inserts a code for the specified element. The page number code is &[Page]. In the right header box in Figure 9.1, you can see that I first typed some text and then clicked Current Date to insert the &[Date] element. You can select the text and element codes in a header or footer box and use formatting choices on the Home tab to adjust the formatting. To finish your entry in a header or footer box, click another box. (If you press Enter, that just creates a line break within the box.)

To insert a picture such as a logo that you want to print on every page, click the Picture button in the Header & Footer Elements group, and then use the choices in the Insert Pictures dialog box to select and insert a picture. The &[Picture] code then appears in the box, and when you click another header or footer box to finish the entry, the picture appears on the page.

Presets available
in this group

Individual elements to insert
available in this group

Header & Footer tab

| File | Home | Insert | Page Layout | Formulas | Data | Review | View | Help | Header & Footer | | ☁ Share | 💬 Comments | 🙂 |

Header & Footer | Page Number | Number of Pages | Current Date | Current Time | File Path | File Name | Sheet Name | Picture | Format Picture | Go to Header | Go to Footer |

☐ Different First Page   ☑ Scale with Document
☐ Different Odd & Even Pages   ☑ Align with Page Margins

Header & Footer   Header & Footer Elements   Navigation   Options

A22

Header

Print Date: &[Date]

	2DAY TECH										
1			**First Half Payroll**								
2			**2Day Tech Services, LLC**								
3											
4	Location	January	Februar	March	April	May	June	Total	Average	
5	N. Charlotte	$61,994	$61,689	$60,654	$73,690	$61,721	$51,680	########	######	
6	S. Charlotte	67,080	57,602	63,437	72,441	72,458	68,037	########	######	
7	Winston-Salem	63,364	69,701	50,541	71,780	66,321	59,296	########	######	
8	Greensboro	56,366	68,436	71,936	66,947	67,247	51,614	########	######	
9	Total	$248,804	$257,428	$246,568	$284,858	$267,747	$230,627	########	$256,005	
10										

Inserted logo
(picture graphic)

Typed text and
&[Date] code

9.1 The choices on the Header & Footer tab enable you to build header and footer components.

> **Genius**
>
> If an inserted picture looks too big, reselect the &[Picture] code in the header or footer box, and then choose Header & Footer ➔ Header & Footer Elements ➔ Format Picture. The Format Picture dialog box that appears includes settings for sizing, cropping, and more on its three tabs. Or use a graphics program to resize a copy of the picture file, and then reinsert it into the header or footer. For a logo, a file that's .5 inches high usually fits.

When Page Layout view shows you that the document will be multiple pages, you can check the Different First Page and Different Odd & Even Pages check boxes to set up additional headers and footers.

To finish working with the header and footer, click outside the header or footer area, in the margin or on a cell. You can choose View ➔ Workbook Views ➔ Normal to change back to Normal view. To edit a header or footer, choose Insert ➔ Text ➔ Header & Footer or View ➜ Workbook Views ➜ Page Layout again. Click in the header or footer box to edit, make the desired changes, and click another box to finish as before. You can edit text, delete element codes, add new elements, and so on.

Note After you work with or view headers and footers in Page Layout view, when you go back to Normal view, you may see a dashed line over a regular gridline. This indicates a page break.

When you're working with a chart sheet and choose Insert ➜ Text ➜ Header & Footer, the Page Setup dialog box opens, with the Header/Footer tab displayed. You also can display this dialog box by clicking the dialog box launcher in the Page Setup group of the Page Layout tab and then click the Header/Footer tab. As shown in Figure 9.2, you also can choose Header or Footer presets from drop-down lists or use the Custom Header or Customer Footer button to open a dialog box where you can insert elements in the three sections. Click OK as needed when you finish using the dialog box(es) to set up the header or footer.

9.2 The Header/Footer tab of the Page Setup dialog box also has header and footer presets.

Changing Page Settings

Like other programs that create various types of documents, Excel has default settings for various aspects of the document. Margins, orientation, paper size, and scaling settings are most important, so I'll focus on those. The Page Setup group of the Page Layout tab enables you to make these page changes.

Margins

The margins are the white areas between the data and the edges of the printed page. Excel's default preset for this is Normal, which allows for .75-inch margins at the top and bottom and .7-inch margins at the left and right. You can use one of two methods to change margins:

- **Choose a preset.** In the Page Setup group of the Page Layout tab (see Figure 9.3), click the Margins button, and then choose one of the available presets from the gallery.

9.3 The Margins button in the Page Setup group enables you to apply a preset or display detailed margins settings.

● **Use the Margins tab of the Page Setup dialog box.** Choose Page Layout ➜ Page Setup ➜ Margins ➜ Custom Margins. The Page Setup dialog box opens with the Margins tab displayed, as shown in Figure 9.3. Adjust the settings in the four margin text boxes as needed. Another advantage to using the dialog box is that you also can adjust the vertical area for headers and footers in the Header and Footer text boxes. When you finish, click OK to apply the changes.

Caution Most printers have minimum margin sizes. Check your printer specs to ensure that you don't set margins that are too small, which can cause data to be cut off in the printout or even produce error messages.

Orientation and paper size

Orientation determines the layout of the page. Portrait, the default, means the page is taller than it is wide. Landscape means that the page is wider than it is tall. Sometimes, sticking with the default works. For example, invoice templates and designs traditionally arrange the sheet information in a vertical arrangement meant to fit a standard letter-sized (8.5" x 11") page in portrait orientation. In other cases, you might have many more columns of data than rows, where changing to the wider landscape orientation might save some pages in the printout.

To change orientation, choose Page Layout ➜ Page Setup ➜ Orientation ➜ Landscape or Page Layout ➜ Page Setup ➜ Orientation ➜ Portrait.

Note I'm not going to be a broken record and repeat that you can use the Page Setup group dialog box launcher to open the dialog box and then select the desired tab to access many of the settings described here in the middle part of the chapter, including the page orientation settings. The Scale to Fit and Sheet Options group dialog box launchers on the Page Layout tab also open the Page Setup dialog box.

The paper size relative to the data also might impact your choice of whether to use a portrait or landscape orientation. For example, if your printer can handle the 8.5" x 14" legal paper size, a landscape orientation might help all the data in a sheet print on a single, wider page. Use the Size button in the Page Setup group of the Page Layout tab to choose another paper size.

Scaling

True story: I find scaling a printout to be one of the most useful page layout settings. It's annoying when a stray row or column prints on (and wastes) a whole separate piece of paper. Plus, it opens up the possibility of losing that extra page and the information it presents, creating an incomplete picture of your data. I often scale a worksheet printout to restrict it to a single page. Or, you might have a printout that you think can fit to a couple of pages wide and one page tall but want to make sure that that happens.

The Scale to Fit group of the Page Layout tab contains the scaling settings. In Figure 9.4, I've selected 1 Page from the Width and Height drop-down lists to restrict the printout to one page wide by one page tall. Notice that this disables the Scale setting.

9.4 Scale the printout to a set number of pages or a percentage.

If you try to make a printout scale to a larger number of pages but there isn't enough data to fill those pages, Excel won't scale the document. Instead, you can try increasing the Scaling setting to something like 125% or 150%, but be advised that this scales the font size of the sheet contents rather than just redistributing some of the sheet contents to an additional page or pages.

Just as paper size and page orientation can be somewhat related, your scaling choices may be impacted by any print area specified in the sheet. See the later section called "Setting a print area" to learn more.

Changing Sheet Settings

Beyond working with the page settings for a printout, you can control some aspects of how the content appears within the printed area of the sheet. Further refining the page design in this way can make the printout easier to follow.

Adding print titles

Print titles are rows or columns that repeat on every page of a printout. (Yes, this is a whole different thing than freezing rows and columns on-screen, covered in Chapter 2.) Specifying print titles helps readers know what the rows and columns of data mean, no matter which page of a printout they're looking at.

Follow these steps to set up print titles for a sheet:

1. **Choose Page Layout → Page Setup → Print Titles.** The Page Setup dialog box opens with the Sheet tab selected.

2. **Under Print Titles, use the Rows to Repeat at Top and/or Columns to Repeat at Left text boxes to select the print titles.** You can type in references if you want, but they have to be absolute references to the column letters or row numbers only (recall that you use the $ for absolute references). These text boxes have the collapse and expand buttons at the right, but I've found that you can just click in one of the text boxes and click a column header/row number (or drag to select multiple columns or rows), and the dialog box will collapse and expand automatically. In Figure 9.5, I've specified both types of print titles.

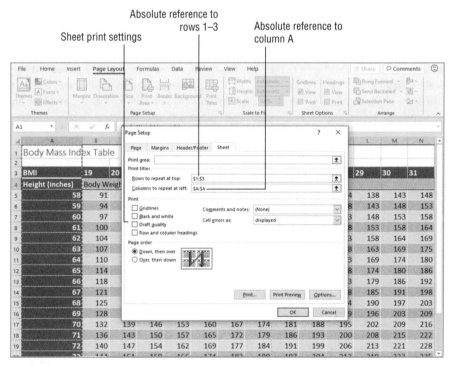

9.5 Specify print titles to repeat on every page of a multipage printout.

3. **Click OK.**

Genius

Some of the settings you choose for printing—such as print titles and the print area—can be saved with the file so you don't have to make those selections again in the future. After applying those settings, use your old friend Ctrl+S to save the settings in the file.

Controlling whether gridlines and other features print

A lot of people overlook these settings, but they can make an important difference in the appearance of your printout. If you look at the Sheet Options group of the Page Layout tab, as shown in Figure 9.4, by default the View check box is checked for both Gridlines and Headings (column and row headers), but the Print check boxes are not. I assume this is because cell gridlines and the headers make it easier to build formulas, but they aren't so useful on a sheet printout.

Caution

Sheet formatting can override printed gridlines in some instances. If you have a worksheet with a table or other range that has white borders for cells, printing gridlines will not cause those borders to turn black. To have printed black borders, you'd have to change the table style or border formatting in the range.

That said, there are times when you might want to print gridlines and headings in a printout. A good example is if you choose Formulas ➔ Formula Auditing ➔ Show Formulas and then want to make a printout with the displayed formulas. Including the gridlines and headings would give the formulas more context in the printout.

So, to print the Gridlines and Headings (column and row headers), just click to check the Print check box under each in the Sheet Options group of the Page Layout tab. If you refer to Figure 9.5, the Sheet tab of the Page Setup dialog box also includes a Print section, where you can control not only the printing of gridlines and headings, but also other aspects such as comments, notes, and errors.

Working with Page Breaks

When you print, Excel initially assumes you want to print all of the sheet contents, and it makes its best guess about what area to print and where to break between pages. To be honest, some of its guesses can be, well, *awkward* (as a typical teenager might say). You can override those best guesses with better choices by setting the print area and adjusting page breaks.

Setting a print area

The print area is self-explanatory, really. I find that I usually set a print area when my sheet has other contents, such as reference information or an extra table, that I don't need to see in my printout. Or, you might have a project estimate sheet where you want to print the actual estimate portion, but not the detailed calculations further to the right on the sheet, because your client doesn't need those added details.

I'm covering this feature along with page breaks because the specified print area contributes to determining the number of pages and page breaks in the printout. To limit the printout to a specific area to print, select the range and then choose Page Layout ➜ Page Setup ➜ Print Area ➜ Set Print Area. To clear a print area that you've selected previously, choose Page Layout ➜ Page Setup ➜ Print Area ➜ Clear Print Area.

Caution Carefully review the print preview when you've selected a print area. You want to make sure you didn't leave anything out or include sensitive information that's for your eyes only.

Vertically and horizontally centering the contents of each printout page (see Figure 9.6) adds another dash of professionalism, and it's more important when the sheet contents or contents of the selected print area don't fill the entire page(s). Excel by default jams the printed contents into the upper-left corner of the page. To fix this and even out the white space, check the Horizontally and Vertically check boxes under Center on Page on the Margins tab of the Page Setup dialog box. (Refer to Figure 9.3.)

Viewing and moving breaks

At last I get to talk about Page Break Preview view! This view simply provides a visual method for adjusting page breaks. To display Page Break Preview, choose View ➜ Workbook Views ➜ Page Break Preview. The zoom of the sheet changes and blue page break lines appear, along with a gray "watermark" label for each page. The solid blue lines indicate manual page breaks or breaks resulting from being the bottom- or far-right boundary of the sheet data or selected print area. The dashed lines are page breaks suggested by Excel.

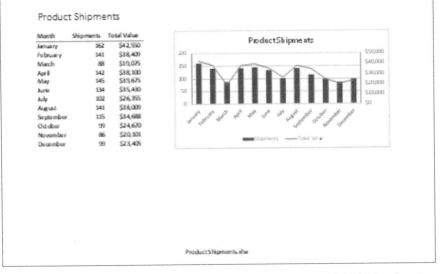

Product Shipments

Month	Shipments	Total Value
January	162	$42,550
February	141	$38,409
March	88	$19,075
April	142	$38,100
May	145	$39,675
June	134	$35,430
July	102	$26,355
August	141	$38,009
September	115	$34,688
October	99	$24,670
November	86	$20,101
December	99	$23,405

9.6 Vertically and horizontally centering page content yields a more polished printout.

To change a break, move your mouse over the blue line until it changes to a black double-headed arrow pointer, as shown in Figure 9.7. Drag the break to a new position. When you finish, choose View ➔ Workbook Views ➔ Normal to change back to the Normal view.

Note

The Breaks button in the Page Setup group of the Page Layout tab offers a menu of choices for inserting, removing, and resetting all page breaks. You can give this method a shot, but for me, Page Break Preview works in a more intuitive way.

Page Break
Preview button   Page number

Dragging a
page break

File | Home | Insert | Page Layout | Formulas | Data | Review | View | Help | Share | Comments

Default | Normal | Page Break Preview | Page Layout | Custom Views | Ruler | Gridlines | Formula Bar | Headings | Zoom | 100% | Zoom to Selection | New Window | Arrange All | Freeze Panes | Switch Windows | Macros

Sheet View | Workbook Views | Show | Zoom | Window | Macros

AG23 | f_x | 410

Body Mass Index Table

9.7 You can drag a page break to a new position in Page Break Preview view.

Previewing a Printout and Printing

If you've now viewed the Page Setup dialog box a few times, you may have noticed that it includes both Print and Print Preview buttons on every tab. This strikes me as an anachronism that might go away in later versions of Excel, because the previewing and printing functions have been merged over time. Despite that, I think that some method of changing between page setup settings and preview/print settings will always be available, because it's typical to have to tweak settings and preview multiple times until you get the printout to look the way you want.

If you click Print or Print Preview in the Page Setup dialog box, or choose File → Print, or press Ctrl+P, the Print screen of the File tab (Backstage view) appears, as shown in Figure 9.8. The print settings appear below Print in the middle part of the screen, with the preview of the first page at the right. If the printout has multiple pages, the information at bottom center shows you the number of pages. You can use the Next Page and Previous Page buttons to navigate between the pages to review them carefully. Clicking the Zoom to Page button at the lower right zooms in for closer examination, and clicking the button a second time zooms back out. The Show Margins button toggles the display of margin lines in the preview. Drag a margin line to a new position to resize the margin. Black boxes or handles also appear across the top to show the column widths. Dragging one of those resizes the column.

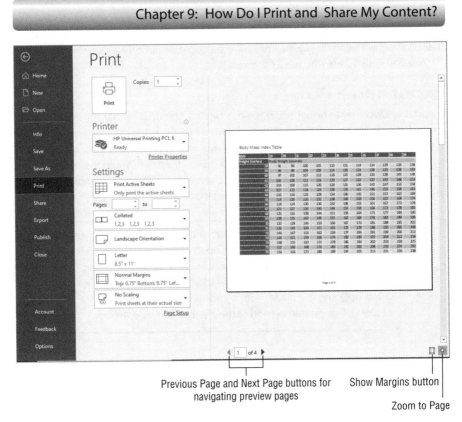

Previous Page and Next Page buttons for   Show Margins button
navigating preview pages

Zoom to Page

9.8 The preview appears with the Print settings.

At the top of the Print settings, you can change the Copies entry to print more copies. Choose the Printer to use from the Printer drop-down list. (It must be turned on, have paper, and so on.) The other choices under Settings largely give you a chance to revisit page settings covered earlier, with the exception of the top two. You can choose to Print Entire Workbook or Print Selection rather than Print Active Sheets, or you can specify a range of Pages to print.

When it all looks good, click the Print button at the top. With any luck, your printer spits out the page(s).

Other Ways to Share Information

You don't *have* to print your Excel information on your end. You may need to send it to someone else digitally so that they can print it. (And please, don't even talk to me about snail mailing or faxing. So 1990s.) You have a couple of options for sharing your Excel information with others who need to review it.

Exporting a PDF

A Portable Document Format (PDF) file has been a standard format for sharing documents for decades now. You can open and print a PDF file using the free Acrobat Reader app, Word, web browsers such as Microsoft Edge and others, and any number of other programs. You can export information from your Excel file to a PDF and then email or otherwise share that PDF with others who need to view and print it. For example, you might export an Excel invoice to a PDF and then email that PDF to your client.

Caution

While a saved PDF no longer has formulas, that doesn't necessarily mean the recipient can't edit it. Word can open a PDF file and convert it to editable text, and the full version of Adobe Acrobat is made for editing PDFs. If you send out a PDF with financial calculations such as an invoice with a total or the supporting calculations for a contract, make sure to verify the contents of any PDF or printed version of the file that you receive back.

Follow these steps to export a PDF file from Excel:

1. **If needed, set a print area or select the range to export on the sheet.** This is another instance where you want to make sure you're not exporting any information that you don't intend to share.

2. **Choose File → Export → Create PDF/XPS Document → Create PDF/XPS.** The Publish a PDF or XPS dialog box appears. It looks similar to the Save As dialog box but has PDF selected as the Save as Type choice by default and includes a couple of other PDF-specific settings.

3. **Navigate to the desired save location and edit the filename as needed.**

4. **If you selected the area to export in Step 1, click the Options button; otherwise, skip to Step 6.** The Options dialog box shown in Figure 9.9 appears.

5. **Under Publish What, click the Selection option button, and then click OK.**

6. **Click Publish.** Your PDF is now ready to email to anyone who needs it! By default, the Open File After Publishing check box in the Publish as PDF or XPS dialog box is checked, as shown in Figure 9.9. This means that after you click Publish, the file opens in the default PDF viewer on your system. This can be Microsoft Edge on a Windows 10 system or another app such as a version of Adobe's Acrobat Reader that's set as the default.

7. **Review the PDF contents for accuracy and then close the PDF viewer app.**

Selection option
button

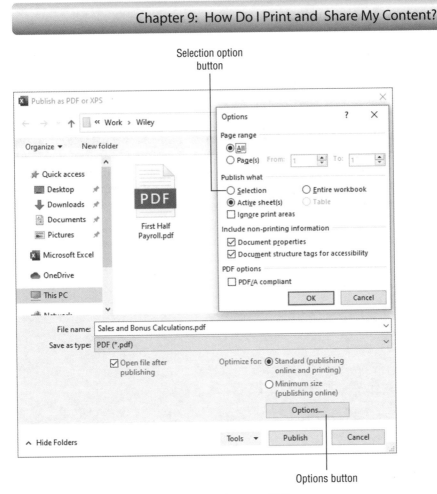

Options button

9.9 You have options when exporting your sheet to a PDF.

Using OneDrive

From this person's perspective, Microsoft seems to be increasingly nudging users to save files to their computers' local OneDrive folders so that the files sync to the user's OneDrive account in the cloud. I get it, it's a no-brainer backup method that can save people from themselves. It can stink for some people, however, because if you have limited data for your Internet connection, all that syncing can chew up a data plan quite quickly.

Setting that little gripe aside, once an Excel file has synced to your OneDrive cloud account or you've uploaded it yourself, you can share it from there. In your web browser, sign on to your OneDrive account and navigate to the folder holding the file, if needed. Select the file, and then click Share in the bar at the top. Choose sharing settings. From there, enter a contact name or email address and click Send to send the sharing list, or click Copy Link and then copy the link so that you can email it to recipients as needed.

Thank You, Reader!

Thank you for grabbing your copy of *Excel Portable Genius* and for staying engaged through the end of the book. I hope it serves as a useful guide as you hone your Excel skills and progress through your career. Sending thoughts of appreciation your way.

Index

A

accessing help, 8
Accounting number format, 94–95
active cell, 7
adding
    background images, 146
    calculated columns, 171–173
    comments to cells, 33
    logos, 146
    print titles, 201–203
    SmartArt graphics, 141–143
    text to shapes, 128–129
    total rows, 173–174
    worksheets, 25–26
addition (+) operator, 61
Align Center button, 104, 134
Align Left button, 104
Align Middle button, 134
Align Right button, 104
alignment
    applying formatting, 103–105
    working with, 134–135
applying
    alignment formatting, 103–105
    font formatting, 100–103
area chart, 179
arguments
    defined, 74
    optional, 79
arithmetic operators, 60

arranging lists in Excel, 150–152
Artistic Effects gallery, 131
assigning multiple range names, 47–48
at (@) operator, 62
AutoCorrect feature, 18, 35
AutoFill, 38–41
AutoFormat feature, 35
AutoSum
    using in formulas, 83
    using on Home or Formulas tab, 74–77
AVERAGE function, 74, 75

B

bar chart, 179
bitmap graphics, 138
borders, working with, 105–106
Bottom Align button, 103
Breaks button, 205
bubble chart, 180

C

Calculator app, 65
callout, 122
Cancel button (Formula bar), 32
capitalization, for functions, 78
CC (Creative Commons), 124
cell address
    changing type of in formulas, 66–67
    defined, 16, 22